MW01027457

WHAT CHRISTIANS NEED TO KNOW ABOUT THE QURAN AND ISLAM

A Doctrinal Comparison of the Quran to the Bible

The Cross of Jesus Christ Compared to The Crescent Moon of Allah!
Biblical Grace Compared to Qur'anic Works!
Killed for sharing the Gospel Compared to Killing for Allah!
Christian belief Compared to Muslim belief!

BY JOHN J. ISAIAS

PREFACE

The world we live in today is in tremendous turmoil over religion. The manifestation of brutal murders in the form of car and truck bombings, suicide bombings, mass shootings, and beheadings are common. The central theme surrounding these events is that of the religion of Islam. Arguments persist as to the motivation and context of those committing the acts of terror. Arguments over defining the atrocities as terrorism, radical terrorism, radical Islamic terrorism, and even workplace violence have filled the news. Depending on the reporting, different definitions are given. One news outlet will have a person railing against ISIS, Hezbollah, Al-Qaeda, Hamas, and other Islamic militants while another will have some Muslim railing about Islamic phobia and touting Islam to be a religion of peace. So, how would one sort through all the spin and political correctness to understand the fundamental truth?

First of all, those perpetrating the atrocities have been almost exclusively Muslim. Internationally, government reports, news reports, and lists of Islamic terrorist attacks over the last twenty years validate the exclusivity. Domestically, the 9/11 attack, the Fort Hood shooting, the Sam Bernardino shooting, the Orlando gay bar shooting, and the Boston Marathon bombing were all Islamic inspired. Second, Christians have not been a part of the turmoil, but have been a prime target for many of the murders and genocide that have taken place. Third, Jews have also been targets, not instigators. Fourth, the non-religious pedestrian activity of any kind of terrorism, however it is defined, pales in comparison to the acts of Islamic-inspired terrorism.

So, what is the common thread that could give insight into the motivation of this type of cruelty? First, you have to look at what is being taught and the commonality of the teachings. There are two major sources of teaching in the Muslim faith. First is the Quran. All Muslims accept this as their sacred text, provided by Allah through the angel Gabriel to their prophet Muhammad. Second is the Hadith. These texts include the traditions of their prophet Muhammad, but are not accepted by all Muslims. So, the most accepted text to read and study for insight would be the Quran.

In an attempt to understand the scope and issues involved, the reading and study of an English version of the Quran was undertaken. Then comparisons of the Quranic verses when feasible were compared to biblical verses. This was done because the Quran includes many biblical stories including creation, the Flood, activities of Noah, Abraham, Ishmael, Isaac, the Jews, and Christians to name a few. However, there are so many discrepancies, there is no hope of reconciliation between the accounts. Muslim scholars and most

Muslims will acknowledge the Torah (either the first five books of the Old Testament or the Old Testament) and the Gospels to be part of Allah's word, but do not accept the Bible as we know it today. **Their position is the Bible has been corrupted over time by the Jews and Christians.** What flies in the face of this Muslim position is the discovery of the Dead Sea Scrolls in 1947! All books of the Old Testament except Esther were present in the scrolls. What is even more significant is a thousand years separates the age of the last scrolls used in the current Bible (935 AD) and the Dead Sea Scrolls (200 BC). Yet, no corruption was found. In fact, when total books such as Isaiah were compared word for word and letter for letter, only some different spellings of the same word were found. The authenticity of the Gospels and the New Testament are also attacked by many. Some statements (not necessarily Muslim) are misleading. The statement that 300 to 400 thousand textual variants are found among existing manuscripts are made with no explanation. In fact, seventy-five percent of these variants are spelling. The second largest variant is that of synonyms and word order difference like "the Jesus." When looking at a breakdown of the variants, *no fundamental doctrine* of Christian faith is impacted. This is because most of the New Testament was written in Cornea Greek, a precise language that limits any variation in interpretation.

A good example of biblical and Quranic differences is found in Isaiah 9, John 14, and Surah 23 and Surah 5 of the Quran. Isaiah 9:6 states: "For unto us a child is born, unto us a son is given, and the government shall be upon his shoulder; and his name shall be called Wonderful, Counselor, The Mighty God, the Everlasting Father, the prince of peace."

John 14:6 states: "Jesus saith unto him, 'I am the way, the truth and the life, no man cometh unto the Father but by me.'"

Surah 23:92 states: "Allah has not taken to himself any son, nor is there any god with him; for then each god would have taken off that he created and some of them would have risen up over others; glory to Allah."

Surah 5:79 states "The Messiah, Son of Mary was only a Messenger." There could be no greater differences in doctrine between the Quran and the Bible than to deny the deity of the Messiah in both the Torah (Old Testament) and the New Testament.

The English version of the Koran selected was "The Koran Interpreted" by Arthur John Arberry. This is the most touted of interpretations by scholars. Professor Arberry was Head of the Department of Classics at Cairo University. There he acquired a first-hand knowledge of literary and social conditions in the Islamic Middle East. Between 1947 and 1969, he served as Sir Thomas Adams Professor of Arabic at Cambridge University. In addition to translating the Koran from Arabic to English, he published twenty books in Islamic studies, many dealing with mysticism and poetry. He died in England in 1969.

When comparing the Quran to the Bible, some interesting contrasts emerge:
1. The god of Islam is *not* the same God of the Bible.
2. Salvation in Islam is *not* the same salvation of the Bible.

3. The heaven of Islam is not the same heaven depicted in the Bible.
4. The history recorded in the Quran is not the same history recorded in the Bible.
5. There is absolutely no reconciliation of the Quran to the Bible.
6. There is absolutely no reconciliation of the Muslim to the Jew.
7. There is absolutely no reconciliation of the Muslim to the Christian.
8. The Quran is not a book of peace; nor is the religion of Islam.
9. Muslim assimilation into any other society (European, American, and Oriental) is highly unlikely, if not impossible.
10. Sharia Law is not compatible with democracy or any free society.
11. The Quran and Bible are different in doctrine and truth.

This study was intended to address the basics of doctrinal differences between Christianity and Islam while providing an understanding of why we are seeing a resurgence of Holy War in Muslim society. The study was also undertaken to provide a foundation for Christians to witness to Muslims. Background on the Muslim holy books and Muhammad is first introduced, and then doctrinal topics are presented with the associated biblical context comparisons. Multiple Qur'anic verses are presented so that no doubt can be placed on contextual presentation.

TABLE OF CONTENTS

DEFINITIONS

1. *Allahu Akbar*: An Islamic phrase called *Takbir* in Arabic; meaning "Allah is greater" or "Allah is greatest."
2. Caliphate: An area containing an Islamic steward known as a Caliph. A person considered a religious successor to the Muslim prophet Muhammad. He is the leader of the entire community, country, or nation.
3. Gehenna: Hell; the place of torment for those who are not true Muslims.
4. Hadith: One of the various reports describing the words, actions, or habits of Muhammad.
5. Hijab: describes the act of covering up generally, but is often used to describe the head-scarfs worn by Muslim women.
6. Iblis: Satan, who was a Jinn.
7. Imran: Family of Mary, mother of Jesus. This is not consistent with the Bible.
8. Jinn: Spiritual beings created by Allah from smokeless fire.

9. Kabba: The cube shaped structure in Mecca, Saudi Arabia. The center of the most holy site for Muslims and the direction where Muslims face during their daily prayers.

10. People of the Book: Christians who believe the Bible as inspired by the Holy Spirit and written by men of the God of the Bible. Considered by Muslims as firewood for Gehenna.

11. Koran/Quran: Muslim holy book, sent down by Allah through the angel Gabriel to Muhammad.

12. *Makara*: Arabic word meaning to deceive, delude, scheme, cheat, lie, double-deal, and double-cross.

13. Niqab: a veil worn by Muslim women. It is used to cover the face leaving the area around the eyes clear.

14. Ramadan: Is the holy month of fasting, intro-spection, and prayer for Muslims. It occurs the ninth month of the Islamic calendar. It is observed by fasting from dawn until sunset to commemorate the first revelation of the Quran to Muhammad. It is one of the five pillars of Islam. The month lasts from 29-30 days based on the visual sighting of the crescent moon.

15. Sheba: The Kingdom of Sheba. The kingdom of the Shebeans included the greater part of Yemen. The place that the Queen of Sheba comes from to meet Solomon.

16. Surah: A chapter or book of the Quran

17. Sunnah: The decisions and actions of Muhammad, Prophet of Islam

18. Sunni Muslim: A sect of Islam chose Muhammad's Adviser Abu Bakr to become the first successor to lead the Muslim State or caliphate after Muhammad's death. Leadership based on ability was the Sunni approach. In 2016, there was an estimated 1.5 billion Sunni Muslims.

19. Shiite Muslim: This sect of Islam chose Ali, Muhammad's cousin and son-in-law. Ali and his successors are called Imams who not only lead the Shiites, but are considered to be decedents of Muhammad.

20. *Taqiyya*: Scheming and lying to the unbeliever by a Muslim to advance the cause of Islam.

21. Wide-eyed houris: Virgins who do not age and are given to Muslim men who are martyred when they go to paradise.

22. We, Us: used to identify Allah in many of the Surah verses. Although, Islam and the Quran states Allah is one, "We" and "Us" are used as his pronoun.

COMMON BIBLICAL NAMES USED IN THE QURAN

Aaron	Ishmael	David
Gabriel	Saul	Joseph
Moses	Baal	Jonah
Abraham	Jacob	Korah
Goliath	Solomon	Elijah
Noah	Benjamin	Lot
Adam	Job	Elisha
Isaac	Zachariah	Ezra
Pharaoh	Cain and Abel	
Apostles of Jesus	John the Baptist	
	Mary (mother of Jesus)	

When a comparison is made between the Quran and the Bible relating to the above individuals, there are discrepancies in either detail or context with every person. Some discrepancies are addressed in Chapter XI.

CHAPTER I
WHAT IS THE KORAN
OR QURAN?

While at work on September 11, 2001, I entered the break area to get a soft drink. The break room TV was on and as I glanced at it, I saw an airplane crash into one of the twin towers of the World Trade Center. The sight of those images of destruction and chaos that followed is still etched in my mind. I recalled the images of the US Marine barracks in Beirut, Lebanon that was destroyed in 1982 and the previous World Trade Center bombing in 1993. This time the attack was not over there and it was not an insignificant event causing some building damage and a few deaths. It was not a spur of the moment event. The attack was orchestrated to cause as much death and destruction to Americans as possible. Later, as the news media broadcasted more information as to the nature and extent of the attack, I realized these threats were not going away and this nation could no longer ignore the fundamental reasons for the attacks. Why would men spend months planning and preparing to kill themselves in an effort to kill only innocent people? Neither the World Trade Center nor those who worked in the buildings posed a military threat to anyone. The terrorists did not know the victims and the victims did not know the terrorists. So, why? My desire was to find the answers.

The 9/11/2001 attack was committed in the name of Islam. In fact, while researching Islamic Inspired terrorist attacks, I found from 1983 through 2001, over ninety attacks occurred in thirty-four countries, killing 2,625 and wounding over 4,800.[1] Was this a religion that encouraged this type of behavior or was this a religion being hijacked by extremist groups with a specific agenda? What were the fundamental teachings, beliefs, and doctrine of the followers of Islam and what was the written authority by which they operated? These were the questions I sought to answer.

The questions pointed to two sources of teaching: the Quran and the Hadith. After obtaining a highly-touted translation of the Quran, I began a study that lasted for ten years. Reading, studying, and comparing the Quran and some of the Hadith to the Bible was the path taken. The reasons were most Muslims always spoke of the Quran and the Prophet of Islam, Muhammad. Also, much of the Quran referenced the Bible and the Bible is the source of authority. Research revealed the Quran as the most authoritative word

---

[1]   National Counter Terrorism Center, "Historic timeline (1969-2001)".

for the Muslim, followed by the Hadith. Following is a summary of my findings as they relate to what the Quran means to the religion of Islam and to the Muslim follower.

Quran, Sacred Text of Islam

The name "Quran" is driven from two words: *al-quar,* meaning "to collect" and *qara,* meaning "to recite." The Quran is the sacred text of Islam, divided into 114 chapters or Surahs, revered as the word of Allah, dictated to Muhammad by the archangel Gabriel, and accepted as the foundation of Islamic law, religion, culture and politics. Some of the Surahs were written in Medina and some were written in Mecca. This seemed logical. However, I chose to go directly to the Quran to seek a self-definition rather than rely on some definition from a source that was prone to spin. What did the source of authority say?

The best definitions, illustrations, and explanations of the Quran come from the Quran itself:

1. Surah 20:110 (page 347): We have sent it down as an Arabic Koran.
2. Surah 2:183 (page 52): wherein the Koran was sent down to be guidance to the people, and as clear signs of the guidance and the salvation.
3. Surah 7:204 (page 196): And when the Koran is recited, give you ear to it and be silent; haply so you will find mercy.
4. Surah 10:37 (page 229): This Koran could not have been forged apart from Allah, but it is a confirmation of what is before it, and a

distinguishing of the Book (Bible), wherein is no doubt, from the Lord of all being.

5. Surah 12:2 (page 254): Those are the signs of the manifest Book we have sent it down as an Arabic Koran haply you will understand.

6. Surah 17:10 (page 303): Surely this Koran guides to the way that is straightest – good for believers; painful chastisement for the unbelievers.

7. Surah 17:46 (page 307): When thou recitest the Koran, *We* place between thee, and those who do not believe in the world to come a curtain obstruction, and *We* lay veils upon their hearts lest they understand it, and in their ears heaviness.

8. Surah 17:90 (page 312): Say: "If men and Jinn banded together to produce the like of this Koran, they would never produce its like not though they backed one another."

9. Surah 27:1 (page 76): Those are the signs of the Koran and a manifest book, a guidance, and good tidings, unto the believers who perform the prayer, and pay the alms, and have sure faith in the hereafter.

10. Surah 27:77 (page 83): Surely this Koran relates to the children of Israel most of that concerning which they are at variance.

11. Surah 27:94 (page 84): I have been commanded to be of those that surrender and to recite the Koran.

12. Surah 34:30 (page 134): The unbelievers say, "we will not believe in this Koran, nor in that before it."
13. Surah 36:2-5 (page 144): By the wise Koran, thou art truly among the envoys on a straight path the sending down of the All-mighty and All-Wise.
14. Surah 41:1 (page 185): A sending down from the merciful, the compassionate a Book whose signs have been distinguished as an Arabic Koran.
15. Surah 41:25 (page 187): The unbelievers say "do not give ear to this Koran, and talk idly about it haply you will overcome" so *We* shall let the unbelievers taste a terrible chastisement.
16. Surah 73:2-4 (page 308): O thou enwrapped in thy robes. Keep vigil the night, except a little (a half of it, or diminish a little, or add a little), and *chant the Koran* very distinctly.
17. Surah 73:20-25 (page 309): Therefore recite of the Koran so much as is feasible. He knows that some of you are sick, and others journeying in the land, seeking the bounty of Allah and others fighting in the way of Allah. So recite of it so much as is feasible. And perform the prayer, and pay the alms, and lend to Allah a good loan.

The verses illustrated above provide the encouragement to the Muslim to accept the Koran as the last and final word from Allah. It will be a blessing to the

Muslim believer and a chastisement to those who do not believe it to be inspired. Its characteristics are:

1. It was sent down from Allah.
2. It is an Arabic Koran giving special significance to the genealogy of Ishmael.
3. Neither man nor Jinn (spiritual being) or both could have composed the book.
4. The Koran is good for those who believe in it and bad for those who do not.
5. It relates to the Jews who do not accept it.
6. Signs are used as significant events to lead humanity to Allah.
7. The Koran is to be chanted and recited by the Muslim.

Signs are mentioned numerous times in the Quran with only signs coming from the Bible (the Flood, Egyptian plagues) validated. No signs are presented that would establish the Quran as authoritative. The puzzling conclusion is the Quran is presented as the final authority of the god of creation, yet not one distinguishing sigh outside of the Bible is presented. How can one discard the Bible with so many of its prophecies already fulfilled and validated as it is written today to accept a text with no validation? Islam accepts the Old Testament and the Gospels as provided to Muhammad by Gabriel, not the Torah of the Jews and the Bible of the Christians. The Muslims believe Jews and Christians have corrupted the Torah and the Bible.

Major Themes Presented in the Quran

The major themes are scattered throughout the Surahs and are repeated multiple times and in different contexts. In a single Surah, you may see multiple themes. For example, in the Second Surah entitled "The Cow," the wilderness wandering of the Jews, the unbelieving Christians and Jews, the Covenant of Allah with Abraham and Ishmael, the construction of the Kaaba by Abraham and Ishmael, Ramadan, divorce, David and Goliath, and Solomon are mentioned. Muhammad rightly said how the unbeliever in Islam viewed the Quran in Surah 21:5: "Nay, but they say: 'A hotchpotch of nightmares! Nay, he has forged it; nay, he is a poet!'"

The list of major themes follows:

➢ **The creation of the universe by Allah.** The creation is listed as a major sign for the believer in Islam. Allah creates the heavens and the earth in six days and sits down to conduct the affairs. What the affairs are is not specific.

➢ **The spiritual world is made up of angels, Satan, and Jinn.** Jinn are spirituals beings made by Allah from smokeless fire. Satan of the Quran is not depicted as the Satan of the Bible. The Satan of the Quran appears to be closely related to the pre-Islamic worship of spiritual beings by the Bedouin Tribes.

➢ **The Arab Muslims are Allah's chosen people. Israel is totally abandoned by Allah** and replaced by the Muslims. Israel is not Allah's chosen people; the Arabs are the chosen people. The abandonment is first mentioned and illustrated when Allah through Moses instructs Israel to sacrifice a cow that has had calves. This has never been an instruction from the God of the Bible. The Levitical system is specific as to the type of acceptable sacrifice and a cow is not one of them.

➢ **Allah's covenant with Abraham and Ishmael as prophets of Islam**. This includes the building of the Kabba by Abraham and Ishmael in Mecca and the teaching that Abraham was a Muslim.

➢ **Jesus, son of Mary, created by Allah**. Jesus is not presented as deity. He is presented as only a messenger, who is less in status before Allah than Muhammad.

➢ **Prophets of Islam**. Most of these are men of the Bible. Discrepancies abound between what the Quran says concerning these prophets (Adam, Noah, Abraham, Ishmael, Isaac, Jacob, Lot, Joseph, Solomon, and Jesus) and what the Bible says.

➢ **Muhammad the last Messenger, Prophet, and spokesman from Allah**. His words are authoritative over all other prophets and prophecies. Any discrepancies between the Bible and the Quran are considered to be corruption imposed by the Jew and Christian.

➢ **Signs as the authenticator of Allah and Muhammad**. No signs outside of the Bible and nature are given. Some of the signs are: Creation, the Flood in Noah's day, the

Egyptian plagues, destruction of Sodom, plant growth, crop yield, rain, birds flying, lighting, ships floating on the sea, night and day, sun and moon, change in wind direction, and the variety of tongues (languages)

➢ **Jews and Christians: the Worst of Beast**. Jews and Christians are not to be befriended. They are deserving of death and should be killed by cutting off their head and fingers. Christians will be judged by Jesus at the resurrection and sent to hell.

➢ **Instructions on daily living**. This includes marriage, divorce, hygiene, and dietary law.

➢ **Benefits of being a martyr**. Paradise is the reward with lots of young women, food and drink.

➢ **Obedience to Muhammad**. Obedience to Muhammad is just as important as obedience to Allah.

There are two major themes repeated over and over in the Quran. The first deals with Jesus son of Mary. Allah has not taken to himself a son. Allah created Jesus. He is not a god, and he is not divine. The second deals with the signs, most of which are listed above. Believers in Allah and Muhammad accept the signs as coming from Allah. The unbelievers do not, but cry lies to the signs as being authentication of Allah, Muhammad, and the other messengers.

CHAPTER II
WHAT IS A HADITH?

After reading the Quran and researching the differences in Muslim beliefs, the Hadith became front and center. The Hadiths provided the foundation and understanding of why some Muslims sought to kill not only non-Muslims, but fellow Muslims of which both believed and accepted the Quran. This was obvious as the war between Iraq and Iran raged from 1980 through 1988. The war was started by Saddam Hussein, a Sunni Muslim and repelled by Iran, a Shia Muslim country. One could say the motivation was over power, not religion. However, the inspiration to fight was religious. The supreme religious leader of the Islamic Republic of Iran was Ayatollah Khomeini. Ayatollah Khomeini was believed to be a direct descendent of the Muslim prophet Muhammad. The Shia faction accepts the religious authority of the descendants of Muhammad where the Sunni faction accepts leadership based on ability. These differences are emphasized in the acceptance of the various hadiths; the second most authoritative documents used in Islam. They are used to describe and conduct the practice of Islam. A summary follows:

A Hadith is one of the various reports describing the words, actions, or habits of Muhammad. The term comes from the Arabic meaning a "report," "account," or "narrative." Hadiths are second only to the Quran in developing the Islamic science and philosophy of law (Sharia law). Hadiths were evaluated and gathered during the eighth and ninth centuries, generations after Muhammad's death in AD 632 (100-200 years later). Hadiths are classified as "authentic," "good," and "weak." Acceptance of different Hadiths separates the beliefs of the Sunni and Shia Muslims.

Hadiths are divided into five different schools:

1. Sunni, which consists of six books.
2. Shia, which consists of four books.
3. Ibads: canonical collection Tarib al-Musad.
4. Ahmadiyya, which adopts the six Sunni books.
5. Quranists who reject the authority of the Hadith.

The reason there is such a divergence of adoption is numerous Hadiths appeared during their writing period that were the opposite of each other in instruction. One sect of Islam would write a Hadith that benefited either their political, social, or religious position while another sect would counter with opposite points of view. Both were supposed to be the actual words, actions, or habits of Muhammad.

Some Hadith reports will be used in this document to bridge the gap between the Quran and what

Muslims practice today in Islam. The most prominent Hadith referenced in the topics that follow come from Sahih al-Bukhari. This is one of the six major Hadith collections of Sunni Islam and is widely accepted by most Muslims. The collection was made by the Muslim scholar Muhammad al-Bukhari, who took generations of orally transmitted reports on the Muslim prophet Muhammad and composed them into written documents. He finished the composition work around AD 846. Al-Bukhari traveled throughout the Abbasid Caliphate (the third Islamic caliphate to succeed Muhammad) whose capital was in what today is modern day Baghdad, Iraq gathering the traditional stories.[2],[3]

The Quran mentions the resurrection of the dead and the final judgment that follows in many Surahs. However, the Quran is mostly silent in presenting events that lead up to the final days. The minor and major signs leading up to the last days can be found in various Hadiths. Some of the events covered in the Hadith are the return of the twelfth Imam and Jesus, Son of Mary, who will force the world to become Muslim as well as the appearance of the Muslim antichrist. Some Hadith resources accepted by both Sunni and Shia Muslims will be used to provide an understanding of the Islamic view of Muhammad's

---

[2]   Shaykh al-Hadith 'Allama Ghulam Rasul Saidi, trans. 'Allamah Ishfaq Alam Qadri and M. Iqtidar "Imam Bukhari (194-265)".

[3]   Mohamed Okasha, "Al Bukhari: The Imam of Hadith and Sunnah".

authority and relation to Allah, the end times, and the last battle and the judgment.

Both the Quran and many Hadiths center on Muhammad, the prophet of Islam as much as they do around Allah, the god of Islam. Both Muhammad and Allah are presented in the context of what the Quran and the Hadith say.

CHAPTER III
WHO WAS MUHAMMAD,
PROPHET OF ISLAM?

The January 7, 2015 attack on the *Charlie Hebdo* satirical newspaper in Paris, France by two Muslim men was due to satirical cartoons of Muhammad. Twelve people were killed and eleven were wounded. The newspaper employee who was forced at gunpoint to let the terrorists into the facility was not killed. The terrorist told her that he would not kill her because she was a woman and that she should read the Quran.[4] By observing the collision between the secular world and the Islamic world in Europe, one sees Muhammad the prophet of Islam as a primary and continuous source of contention.

The growth of Islam in the United States has made Muhammad the prophet of Islam recognizable to almost everyone. In fact, the growth of mosques in

---

[4]   Vivienne Walt, "Meet the woman the Paris Gunman Spared" January 9, 2015.

the US has gone from 1209 mosques in the year 2000 to 2,106 in 2010 and 3,065 in 2015.[5] College campuses have become fertile ground for the circulation of Islamic literature. Media coverage of the positive attributes of Islam has intensified. These combined initiatives have successfully marketed the religion of Islam and its prophet Muhammad. By researching his political, family, military, and religious life, his character, passions and beliefs became obvious. So, who was Muhammad, the prophet of Islam?

The life of the man Muhammad is filled with a host of contradiction regarding him as a holy man. His warlord tendencies, multiple marriages, and ruthless slaying of many who did not accept the religion he preached have been the topic of much scrutiny. Although Muhammad declares portions of the Bible to be Allah's word to him, his writings in the Quran and his words and actions recorded in the Hadith portray him second only to Allah and cannot be reconciled with either the Old Testament (Torah) or the Gospels. Here is a bullet point history of his life:

Brief History of the Life of Muhammad
  ➢ Born AD 570 in Mecca
  ➢ Orphaned; raised by his uncle Abu Talib
  ➢ Worked as a merchant
  ➢ Married at least fifteen times with sexual slaves and many concubines (see list of Muhammad's wives and concubines)

---

[5] Salatomatic. "Mosques and Islamic Schools" 1998- 2016.

> Would retreat to a cave for prayer; said he was visited by the Angel Gabriel in the cave at age forty. There he started receiving revelations from Allah. Three years later, he started preaching:
>   1. Preached God is one
>   2. Complete surrender (Islam) is the only way.
> Migrated to Medina in AD 622:
>   1. Arrived in Medina completely dependent on the hospitality of the three Jewish tribes that lived there alongside the Arabs.
>   2. In less than two years, two of the tribes that had welcomed him, the Banu Qaynuqa and the Banu Nadir were evicted, losing their land and their wealth to the Muslims who had become powerful enough to take it.
>   3. The last tribe, the Banu Quraza, a group of peaceful farmers and merchants, surrendered to Muhammad without a fight. Muhammad beheaded over 800 men and boys and at least one woman and enslaved the women and children. This is referenced in the Quran, Surah 33:26 (page 124):

And He (Allah) brought down those of the People of the Book who supported them from their fortresses and cast terror in their hearts; some you slew, some you made captive. And He bequeathed upon you their lands, their habitations, and their possessions, and a land you never trod. Allah is powerful over everything.

➤ Received little acceptance and met hostility from some of the Meccan tribes.

Battles recorded either in history, the Quran, or the Hadiths include:
1. Battle of Badr: March 13, AD 624. Muhammad took Mecca; this made him a successful Arab leader.
2. Battle of Uhud: March 19, AD 625 at Mount Uhud. The battle again was between the Meccans and the Muslims.
3. Battle of Khabar: AD 629 between Muslims and Jews. Muslims won and allowed the Jews to stay if they gave half their produce to the Muslims.
4. Battle of the Trench: AD 629 between Muslims and Jews.

Well documented are the battles waged by Muhammad and his followers against the Jews. What is imprinted through history into the minds of the Jewish people is the deception that Muhammad used to gain those victories. Politicians from Europe and the United States have tried for years in vain to successfully bring about some peace accord between the Palestinians on the West Bank and the Jews. The Camp David initiative by the US is all but a failure. Even today, the opposition by the Jews to the US and European agreement with Iran on a nuclear ban is viewed by the Jews as one of Islam's greatest deceptive victories over the west.

> Muhammad died in AD 632.[6]

What the Quran Says About Muhammad:

Again, the best source for understanding the Prophet of Islam is to go to the authoritative sources accepted by the Muslim world. The Quran would be the number one source because it was written in Muhammad's lifetime. Several verses from eight Surahs are included:

1. Surah 3:137 (page 91): Muhammad is naught but a messenger; messengers have passed away before him.

2. Surah 33:40 (page 126): Muhammad is not the father of any one of you men, but the messenger of Allah and the *seal of the prophets*.

3. Surah 61:6: "And when Jesus son of Mary said, 'Children of Israel, I am indeed the messenger of Allah to you confirming the Torah that is before me and giving good tidings of a messenger a messenger who shall come after me whose name shall be Ahmad (Muhammad).'"

4. Surah 47:2 (page 220): Those who believe and do righteous deeds and believe in what is sent down to Muhammad and it is the truth from their Lord, He will acquit them of their evil deeds, and dispose their minds aright.

5. Surah 48:30 (page 229): Muhammad is the messenger of Allah, and those who are with

---

[6] Seyyed Hossein Nasr, "Muhammad Prophet of Islam "Encyclopedia Britannica.

him are hard against the unbelievers, merciful one to another.

6. Surah 8:68 (page 205): It is not for any prophet to have prisoners until he make wide slaughter in the land.

7. Surah 9:64 (page 214): Do they not know that whosoever opposes Allah and His Messenger—for him awaits the fire of Gehenna, therein to dwell forever?

8. Surah 66:4 (page 287): Allah is his protector, and Gabriel, and the righteous among the believers; and, after that, the angels are his (Muhammad) supporters.

Muhammad Places Himself Second Only to Allah:

In the early Surahs (Surah 3), Muhammad depicts himself as no more than a messenger. In the latter Surahs (Surah 33 and 61), he is elevated to the position of the "Seal of the Prophets" and prominent over Jesus, son of Mary. Overall, the Quran (written by Muhammad) positions Muhammad as superior to the angels. Although he claims the revelations he received from Allah were through the angel Gabriel, the superiority is demonstrated by the requirement that the angels bow down to Adam (a man, Surah 2:32).

Second, Muhammad claims himself to be a messenger from Allah. Messengers include Isaac, Jacob, Noah, David, Solomon, Job, Joseph, Moses, Aaron, Zachariah, John, Jesus, Elijah, Ishmael, Elisha, Jonah, and Lot (Surah 6: 83-85). Numerous times in the Quran, the edict is to obey Allah and his messenger of which Muhammad proclaims himself to be the chief of messengers. Again, this is proclaimed in Surah 33:40 where Muhammad states he is the Seal of the Prophets, meaning he is the final word on what Allah spoke through all previous prophets and messengers. Any discrepancies (of which there are many) between what the Bible records and what the Quran states is written off by Muslims as being the contamination of the Bible by Jews and Christians.

What the Hadith "Bukhari" says Concerning Muhammad as Intercessor

The second source of authority comes from the hadith. A statement recorded in Bukhari Volume 9, Book 93 is presented. This was written by Bukhari in AD 846 being what Muhammad allegedly said when he was alive. This is widely accepted by Muslims today and is why so much reverence is shown to Muhammad. Today, written articles and speech by any devout Muslim, which includes the name Muhammad, will always be followed by either, "Peace be upon Him" or some sign of extreme reverence. If you were doomed to hell and there was only one person who could get you out of hell, you may also show him reverence. The Bukhari record indicates Muhammad, after the judgment, will be able to get his followers out of hell.

Bukhari Volume 9, Book 93

Muhammad talked to us saying "on the day of resurrection the people will surge with each other like waves, and then they will come to

Adam and say, 'Please intercede for us with your Lord (Allah).' He will say, 'I am not fit for that but you'd better go to Abraham as he is the Khalit of the beneficent.' They will go to Abraham and he will say, 'I am not fit for that but you'd better go to Moses as he is the one to whom Allah spoke directly.' So they will go to Moses and he will say, 'I am not fit for that but you'd better go to Jesus as he is a soul created by Allah and his word.' (Be; and it was) They will go to **Jesus** and he will say, 'I am not fit for that but you'd better go to Muhammad.

They would come to me (Muhammad) and I would say: 'I am for that:' Then I will ask for my Lord's (Allah) permission and it will be given and then he (Allah) will inspire me to praise him with such praise as I do not know now. So, I will praise him with those praises and will fall down, prostrate before him. Then it will be said, 'O Muhammad raise your head and speak, for you will be listened to; and ask for your will be granted (your request) and intercede for your intercession will be accepted.' I will say, 'O lord my followers! My followers!' And then it will be said, "Go and take out of hell (fire) all those who have faith in their hearts, equal to the weight of barley grain. I will go and do so and return to praise him with the same praises and fall down (prostrate) before Allah."

39

This scene is repeated in the Hadith by Muhammad using the faith the size of a small ant and a mustard seed and again with the faith of a small mustard seed. According to this Surah from Bukhari, Muhammad viewed himself as more influential over Allah than Adam, Abraham, Moses, and even Jesus. His influence extends even into the depths of hell, with the ability to petition Allah for removal of some from hell after they were placed there.

Inconsistencies with the Bible

The inconsistencies with the Bible are revealed in two ways. First, Romans 2:11 states: "For there is no respect of persons with God." The same revelation of God's impartiality toward man is shown in Deuteronomy 10:17 and Acts 10:34. The only favor man has with the God of the Bible is through God the Son, the Lord Jesus Christ. This favor is God's grace. "For by grace are ye saved through faith; and that not of yourselves it is the gift of God, not of works, lest any man should boast" (Ephesians 2:8-9).

Second, the Bible is clear concerning once a person is sent to hell, there is no reversal of the sentence for rejecting Jesus Christ as Lord and Savior. Luke 16:19-31 records what Jesus said about the relationship between the beggar Lazarus and the rich man, Lazarus and God, and the rich man and God. Lazarus died and was carried by the angels into Abraham's bosom. The rich man died and in hell he lifted up his eyes tormented in the flame. The rich man petitioned Abraham to send Lazarus to dip his finger in water and place it on his tongue that it might be cooled.

Abraham replied in Luke 16:26, "And beside this, between us and you there is a great gulf fixed, so that they who would pass from here to you cannot; neither can they pass to us that would come from there."

With the combination of the sayings in the Quran and the Hadith, it is no question as to how Muhammad viewed himself and how his followers view him. However, the perceived status is completely contrary to what the Bible states. This self-exaltation explains why Muhammad states in many of the Surahs that true Muslims must obey him, the messenger (Muhammad).

Muhammad's Wives and Concubines:

To further understand who Muhammad the man was is to research his family life and his treatment of women. Muhammad's mindset on women, sex, and marriage is given in two of the Quran Surahs that Muhammad wrote. Women seem to have been for man's pleasure. They were gathered, contracted, married, enslaved, divorced, and dispersed like property. The following Surah verses provide some insight:

1. Surah 65:1 (page 284): "O Prophet, when you divorce women, divorce them when they have reached their period."

2. Surah 65:5 (page 284): "As for your women who have despaired of further menstruating, if you are in doubt, their period shall be three months, and those who have not menstruated as yet." (Note: This Surah is titled "Divorce.")

3. Surah 66:1 (page 287): "O Prophet, why for-biddest thou what Allah has made lawful to thee, seeking the good pleasure of thy wives?"
4. Surah 66:5 (page 287): "It is possible that, if he divorces you, his Lord will give him exchange wives better than you, women who have surrendered, given to fasting, who have been married and virgins too."

Additional insight is provided by the history of Muhammad's wives, concubines, and sexual slaves. Muhammad was married at least fifteen times, he was divorced six times, had at least three sexual slaves, and eleven broken engagement contracts. Muhammad's first wife was a wealthy merchant who proposed and married Muhammad when he was at the age of twenty-four. They had six children and she (Khadijah bint Khuwaylid) was a key player in the earlier development of Islam.[7]

Another notable wife was Aisha bint Abi Bark. She was six years old when the marriage contract was made. She was the daughter of Muhammad's head evangelist Abu Bakr. The marriage was consummated when Aisha was nine years old and remained one of his favorite wives. Aisha was a major contributor to information that comprised Islamic law and history.[8]

Other wives who were significant contributors to the custody of the text of the Quran and teaching of

[7] Allamah Muhammad Baqir, "Wives of the Prophet – their number and a brief account of them" Hayat Al-Qulub Vol.2.
[8] Myriam Francois-Cerrah, "The truth about Muhammad and Aisha" September 17, 2012.

Islamic law were Hafsa bint Umar and Hindbint Abi Umayya. These women appear to have played key roles in helping Muhammad spread the new religion of Islam.

Outside of the marriage to a six-year-old, another marriage that attracted much attention was the marriage of Muhammad to his daughter-in-law, Zaynab bint Jahsh. She was married to Muhammad's adopted son Sayd ibn Harithah and she was also Muhammad's cousin. Muhammad forced his adopted son to divorce her so that he could marry her. He accomplished this by saying he had received new revelations. The two revelations were that an adopted son did not count as a real son, therefore Zaynab was not his real daughter-in-law and as a prophet of Islam, he was allowed more than the customary four wives.

Muhammad divorced six of his wives and considered divorcing at least one other. The one who he considered divorcing and did not was the oldest of his wives, who was intellectually slow, fat, and unattractive. Muhammad married her after his first wife's death at a time when he was unpopular and running out of money. Although he did not divorce here, Sawda bint Zam'a was reduced to no more than a house servant. Another less appealing wife was Amara bint Yazid, who showed signs of leprosy so Muhammad divorced her. Muhammad divorced another wife for peeking at men who frequented the mosque. This wife was condemned to be a dung collector for the rest of her life. Other divorces were the result of the wife finding out that Muhammad was responsible for the death of a family member. Marriage and divorce was of no consequence to Muhammad. Any infatuation toward a woman might result in a marriage and any irritation or inconvenience to him might result in a divorce with consequences to the woman.

Sexual slaves were part of Muhammad's spoils of war, his deception and political presence. He received two sexual slaves as political gifts: one from the Governor of Egypt and another from a friend. He personally selected one of his sexual slaves from the Jewish Qurayza tribe in Medina. These Jews were destroyed by Muhammad's forces, resulting in the beheading of 800 men and boys and enslavement of the women and children. This was the deception of Muhammad after these Jews had befriended him and his followers when they emigrated from Mecca.

In addition to the above marriages, divorces, and sexual slaves, Muhammad was engaged to at least eleven other women. The marriages were not consummated due to a host of reasons.

How does this history of beheadings and sex slaves play out in Islam today? Two of many examples that have filled the news media recently is presented: first, in August 2014, ISIS (Islamic State of Iraq and Syria) fighters committed genocide against the Yazidi people of Sinjar, Iraq. Men and boys were shot or beheaded if they refused to convert to Islam. Girls and women were taken as sex slaves. A Yazidi girl who escaped captivity stated the ISIS fighters told them, "Once we rape you, you will be Muslim."

Second, in April 2014, the Islamic terrorist group Boko Haran abducted 200 young women from a school in Chibok, Nigeria. Many were forced to become sex slaves with others sold. Most have not been heard from. Muhammad's attitude toward women and sex slaves continues to carry over into most of today's Islamic terrorist groups.

From the beginning, the concept of terrorism was Muhammad's method of waging war. The slaughter of innocent Jews at Medina was an early example, while other similar slaughters are carried out in numerous places today. When Muhammad stated in Surah 48:30 that those who were with him should be hard against the unbelievers, he defined harshness in Surah 8:68. "It is not for any prophet to have prisoners until he makes wide slaughter in the land. Take no prisoners until fear is instilled in the hearts and minds of the people". This fear had two objectives: first, to set an example that any opposition would be crushed with the most heinous method of death, beheading, and chopping off fingers. As was in Medina, this wide slaughter today is performed in the presence of family members and friends. The second objective is to force the religion of Islam on those who are being targeted. As was offered to the Yazidi people by the ISIS fighters, if they renounced their religion and pledged their allegiance to Islam, they would be spared from being murdered. This method of spreading Islam during Muhammad's lifetime is still being practiced today. The basis for the second objective is clearly stated in Surah 9:5:

> Then, when the sacred months are drawn away, slay the idolaters wherever you find them, and take them, and confine them, and

lie in wait for them at every place of ambush. But if they repent, and perform the prayer and pay the alms, then let them go their way; Allah is all forgiving, all-compassionate.

The simple equation is convert or be killed.

Muhammad: the Center of Islam in the Quran and the Bible?

Given what the Quran, some Hadiths and current Muslim scholars say about Muhammad's position, what does the Bible say? The Quran's statement in Surah 61:6 that Jesus spoke of Ahmud (Muhammad) coming after him is found nowhere in the Bible. Today's Muslim scholars use John 14 to say Jesus spoke of Muhammad as the comforter and Paraclete. However, it is clear in both John 14 and 16, Jesus is speaking of the coming of the Holy Spirit.

Today's world of Islam attempts to reconcile the Bible with the Quran with Muhammad being the centerpiece. The Institute of Islamic Information and Education declares Muhammad is mentioned many times in the Bible. Their claim is Muhammad was a prophet like Moses and use Deuteronomy 18:18 as their source. The God of the Bible spoke to Moses in verses 15 and 18: "The Lord thy God will raise up unto thee a prophet from the midst of thee, of thy brethren, like unto me; unto him ye shall hearken," The brethren indicates specifically a Jew not an Arab and not Muhammad. Also claimed is Muhammad was the paraclete, comforter, helper and admonisher sent by Allah after Jesus. They use John 14:15-16 as the source. Verse 16 states: "And I will pray the Father, and he shall give you another Comforter, that he may abide with you forever." Verse 17 is conveniently left off, which states: "Even the spirit of truth whom the world cannot receive because it seeth him not, neither knoweth him: but you know him: for he dwelleth with you, and shall be in you." Muhammad was not the spirit of truth; you could see him. He did not dwell among the disciples and was definitely not in the disciples.

Also stated by Muslim authors writing for The Institute is Muhammad will reprove the world of sin and of righteousness and of judgment. Considering the dubious life style of sex slaves, genocide, and deceit, how could this connection be inferred? Further, it is amazing the Muslims can reject the crucifixion, death, burial, and resurrection of Jesus that is clearly given in the Gospel of John and yet use the very scripture in the Bible to try in some way to validate Muhammad to be a special messenger of Allah. However, these assertions are being accepted by many who do not know what the Bible or the Quran says. Consider the number of Muslims throughout the world; this influence is massive and spreading.

Muslims, as of 2010, reached over 1.6 billion: 1.5 billion Sunni and 170 million Shia.[9]

Through year 2015 the Muslim total population was estimated at **1,703,146,000**[10]

---

[9]   Lipka, "Muslims and Islam", Pew Research Center 2016.

[10] Johnson, Zurlo, Hickman and Crossing, "Christianity 2015. Religious Diversity and personal contact" 2015.

CHAPTER IV
WHO IS ALLAH, "THE GOD OF ISLAM"?

Many of the victims and witnesses of the Fort Hood shooting that occurred on November 5, 2009 stated Major Nidal Hasan shouted, "*Allahu akbar*" before using .45 caliber pistols to kill thirteen soldiers and wound over thirty other service men and women. This same shout has been used in many other terrorist attacks across the US and Europe. What does it mean and why would a person use it in the middle of killing others? The words, "*Allahu akbar*" is an Islamic phrase called *takbir* in Arabic, meaning, "Allah is greater" or "Allah is greatest." So, if a person will kill innocent people and possibly die in the process while shouting this phrase, who is this Allah of the Quran? Who would bless and reward one for committing such crimes in his name?

Allah the Creator:
1. Surah 10:3 (page 224): "Surely your Lord is Allah, who created the heavens and the earth in six days, then sat Himself upon the Throne, directing the affair."
2. Surah 4:1 (page 100): "Mankind, fear your Lord, who created you of a single soul, and from it created its mate, and from the pair of them scattered abroad many men and women."
3. Surah 15:16-20 (page 282):

We have set in heaven constellations and decked them out fair to the beholders, and guarded them from every accursed Satan excepting such as listens by stealth-and he is pursued by a manifest flame. And the earth We stretched it forth, and cast on it firm mountains, and We caused to grow therein of everything justly weighed, and there appointed for your livelihood, and for those you provide not for.

4. Surah 15:25 (page 282): "Surely, We created man of a clay and the Jinn created We before of fire flaming."
5. Surah 80:15 (page 324): "Of what did He create him? Of a sperm-drop He created him and determined him, then the way eased for him, then makes him to die, and buries him, then when He wills, He raises him."
6. Surah 3:82 (page 82): "Truly the likeness of Jesus, in Allah's sight is as Adam's likeness; He created him of dust then said unto him 'Be' and he was."

Regarding the creation of man, Surah 15:25 and Surah 80:15 are a contradiction. Did Allah create man from clay or from a sperm-drop? According to the Bible in Genesis 2:7, "And the Lord God formed man of the dust of the ground, and breathed into his nostrils the breath of life; and man became a living being." There was no sperm-drop before Adam was created.

According to the Bible, Jesus was not created. The Gospel of John gives great insight as to the deity and eternity of Jesus Christ. Jesus was not created; He has always been. John 1:1-2 and 14 states: "In the beginning was the Word and the Word was with God, and the Word was God. The same was in the beginning with God. And the Word was made flesh, and dwelt among us (and we beheld his glory, the glory as of the only begotten of the Father), full of grace and truth."

According to the Bible, Jesus was not created; He is the creator! Colossians 1:16-17 states: "For by Him (Jesus) were all things created, that are in heaven, and that are in earth, visible and invisible, whether they be thrones, or dominions, or principalities, or powers-all things were created by him, and for him." There could be no greater difference in the doctrines of the Quran and the Bible as it relates to the deity and eternity of Jesus Christ.

Allah Omnipotent Over His Servants:
Surah 6:61 (page 156): "He is the omnipotent over His servants." Taken in context with the other characteristics of Allah, he is all-powerful and simply does

what he wants to do with mankind. Whereas, the God of the Bible works out his purpose to redeem mankind and orchestrate the things that come into a believer's life for good. The Bible says in Romans 8:28: "And we know all things work together for good to them that love God, to them who are called according to his purpose."

Allah's Binding Obligation:

The phrase, *"Allahu akbar"* is best understood in the context of the only binding obligation that Allah has toward his followers. It is the act of martyrdom in the name of Allah.

Surah 9:112 (page 220): "Allah has bought from the believers their selves and their possessions against the gift of paradise; they fight in the way of Allah; they kill and are killed; that is a promise binding upon Allah in the Torah, and the Gospel and the Koran and who fulfils his covenant truer than Allah?" This verse is the foundation for Islamic martyrdom and the concept of a work that would guarantee paradise. When Major Nidal Hasan shouted the phrase, he was prepared to meet Allah who would be obligated to receive him into paradise.

The Bible States Salvation by Grace, not Works:

The God of the Bible (Old Testament, Torah, New Testament, Gospels) never promises eternal life in heaven for fighting or dying in a cause related to the God of the Bible. In 1 Samuel 2:12, the Bible says: "Now the sons of Eli (the High Priest of Israel) were worthless men; they knew not the Lord." These two men (Hophni and Phinehas) defiled the sacrifices brought by the people and lay with women who assembled at the door of the tabernacle of the congregation. They carried the Ark of the Covenant into battle against the Philistines and were killed. There is no room to interpret these two men who died carrying the symbol of God into battle went to heaven. In fact, God judged the whole house of Eli. It was judged for these two men's transgressions and Eli's failure to disciple them.

In Ephesians 2:5,8-9, the Bible says, "Even when we were dead in sins, hath made us alive together with Christ by grace ye are saved. For by grace are ye saved through faith (in Jesus Christ) and that not of yourselves, it is the gift of God, not of works, least any man should boast." What is claimed in the Quran cannot be reconciled to the Bible. The Quran guarantees one work will result in paradise. The Bible states salvation is by God's grace through faith in the Lord Jesus Christ.

Allah, the Greatest Deceiver

The idea of deceit by Allah is not just viewed as deceit against the non-Muslim; it is of great concern to the believing Muslim. According to the Quran, none of the believers can feel secure (Surah 7:99). The deceit is the major reason for a person to become a martyr. The only assurance of the security of the believer in Islam is to become a martyr. The following verses in the Quran provides the context to Allah's deceit:

1. Surah 3:46 or Surah 3:54 (in some translations page 81): "And they devised (the unbelievers), and Allah devised (against the unbelievers), and Allah is the best of devisers."

2. Surah 7:99 (page 183): "Do they feel secure against Allah's devising? None feels secure against Allah's devising but the people of the lost. Is it not a guidance to those who inherit the earth after those who inhabited it that, did We will, We would smite them because of their sins, sealing their hearts so they do not hear?"

3. Surah 7:181 (page 193): "And those who cry lies to Our signs We will draw them on little by little whence they know not; and I (Allah) respite them –Assuredly My Guile (deceit) is sure."

4. Surah 8:30 (page 200): "And when the unbelievers were devising against thee, to confine thee, or slay thee, or to expel thee, and were devising and Allah was devising; and Allah is the best of devisers."

The Arabic word used for devise or plot is *makara*. *Makara* correctly translated from Arabic means, "to deceive, delude, scheme, cheat, double-cross, double-dealing." According to the root meaning of this word *makara*, Allah is the best at deceiving, scheming cheating and lying. Surah 4:157 (page 123) translated by Arberry and the same verse translated by Yusuf Ali, shed a spotlight on what Allah's deception could mean in the crucifixion of Jesus.

We slew the Messiah, Jesus son of Mary, the Messenger of Allah—yet they did not slay him, neither crucified him, only a likeness of that was shown to them. Those who are at variance concerning him surely are in doubt regarding him; they have no knowledge of him, except the following of surmise; and they slew him not of a certainty—no indeed. (4:157, Arberry)

That they said (in boast): "We killed Christ Jesus the Son of Mary, the Apostle of Allah," but they killed him not, nor crucified him, **but so it was made to appear to them**, and those who differ therein are full of doubts, with no (certain) knowledge, but only conjecture to follow, for of a surety they killed him not (4:157, Yusuf Ali).

The implication in both translations is the event was made to appear that the crucifixion of Jesus took place, when in fact it did not. Who initiated this deceit? Allah initiated the deceit. Allah made the people believe Jesus, son of Mary, died on the cross when he did not. **If this were true,** Allah performed the greatest of all deceptions. Even the enemies of Jesus, the Pharisees, the Roman soldiers, the bystanders, and Pilot as well as the disciples and apostles of Jesus were duped (deceived). The Quran is saying the crucifixion was Allah's deceptive scheme so that people would believe Jesus was crucified when he was not. The consequences, if this were true, are Allah has led astray billions of people by that one deception. This would insure the destination of all witnesses then and many to follow to be hell. If this were true, what deceit!

Even Muhammad and his closest companion Abu Bukr (Muhammad's head evangelist and father-in-law whose daughter Muhammad married at age six) were afraid of Allah's schemes. In one of the Hadiths, Ibn Abbas said: "The prophet (Muhammad) used to supplicate, saying: 'My Lord, aid me and do not aid against me, and grant me victory and do not grant victory over me, plot (scheme/connive/deceive) for me and do not plot (scheme/connive/deceive) against me, guide me and facilitate guidance for me, grant me victory over those who transgress against me.'"

If any doubt remains as to the meaning of the term *makara*, the testimony of Abu Bakr regarding his uncertainty of his status before Allah should seal it: from book one, Abu Bakr has come page 99: "Although he had such a faith, which was too great to suffice all the inhabitants of the earth, he was afraid that his heart might go astray. So, he used to utter, while weeping: 'Would that I have been a bitten tree!' Whenever he was reminded of his position in Allah's sight, he would say: 'By Allah! I would not rest assured and feel safe from the deception of Allah, even if I had one foot in paradise.'"

If the prophet of Islam (Muhammad) and his chief evangelist were afraid of Allah's schemes, shouldn't every Muslim today be even more fearful? Today, this helps to explain better the number of martyrs in the name of Allah seen in today's society. Again, Allah's binding obligation of granting paradise to one murdering in the name of Allah would preclude Allah's scheming and deception.

What the Bible Says About Lying and Deceit

The God of the Bible forbids lying and hates lying. Leviticus 9:11 says, "Ye shall not steal, neither deal falsely, neither lie one to another." Proverbs 6:16-19 says:

> These six things doth the Lord hate; yea, seven are an abomination unto Him: A proud look, **a lying tongue**, and hands that shed innocent blood. A heart that deviseth wicked imaginations, feet that are swift in running to mischief, **a false witness that lies,** and he that soweth discord among brethren.

Proverbs 12:22 says, "Lying lips are an abomination to the Lord, but they that deal truly are His delight." Also, the God of the Bible does not instigate confusion. In 1 Corinthians 14:33, Paul is writing to the church at Corinth dealing with sin in that church body: "For God is not the author of confusion but of peace, as in all churches of the saints." The God of the Bible does not use deceit, misdirection, or any divisive method to accomplish His purpose. Allah's purpose or objective many times is accomplished through deceit where the God of the Bible predetermines His purpose. Here lies a significant difference in theology.

The concept of foreknowledge, predestination, and foreordaining seems to be alien to Allah, the god of the Quran. Allah is reactive and must scheme as his adversary his scheming. A god would only have to do that if he had no knowledge of what the future would bring. This would be the situation if a god were bound by time as man is and must plan, react, and pursue to accomplish the desired outcome. The God of the Bible is truly omniscient in all past, present, and future events. He has foreknowledge of all things in all times in His creation. The God of the Bible is not bound by time because He created time and He can orchestrate His purpose without help from anyone or anything. The concept of foreknowledge is illustrated in Acts 2:23 where Peter the Apostle is preaching at Pentecost and states to the people: "Him (Jesus) being delivered by the determinate counsel and **foreknowledge of God**, ye have taken, and by wicked hands have crucified and slain."

God was not taken by surprise when He offered himself on the cross in the person of Jesus. He chose the time, the place, and the people who would carry out the crucifixion as well as those who would hear the message of redemption on the day Peter preached the Pentecost message. In Ephesians 1:11-12 Paul the Apostle writes: "In whom also we have obtained an inheritance being **predestinated according to the purpose** of him who worketh all things after the counsel of his will, that we should be to the praise of his glory, who first trusted in Christ."

Also, in 1 Peter 1:19-20, the Bible states: "But with the precious blood of Christ, as of a lamb without blemish and without spot, Who verily was **foreordained** before the foundation of the world, but was manifest in these last time for you." Before creation, before there was humanity, God determined what, how, and when He would redeem humanity form sin including these Jews to whom Peter wrote.

In the Bible, the best at scheming and lying is Satan. In John 8:44, Jesus spoke to the Pharisees and said, "Ye are of your father the devil, and the lusts of your father ye will do. He was a murderer from the beginning, and abode not in the truth, because there is no truth in him. When he speaketh a lie, he speaketh of his own; for he is a liar, and the father of it." The actions of Satan are only mirrored by the god of the Quran, not the God of the Bible.

Allah Leads Astray Whomever He Wants:

According to the Quran, Allah leads some people to hell and some to paradise. This again places the believing Muslim in a precarious position. How can a person be sure they are on the right path? These Surah verses provide the context:

1. Surah 16:95 (page 297): "Allah leads astray whom He will, and guides whom He will."

2. Surah 35:9 (page 139): "Allah leads astray whomsoever He will, and whomsoever He will, He guides; so let not thy soul be wasted in regrets for them; Allah has knowledge of the things they work."

3. Surah 74:34 (page 311): "He (Allah) will, and He guides whomsoever He will; and none knows the hosts of thy Lord but He."

4. Surah 48:14 (page 226): "To Allah belongs the kingdom of heavens and of the earth;

whomsoever He will, He forgives, and whom-soever He will He chastises."

How does Allah lead men astray? In Surah 13:42, the Quran states: "Those that were before them devised; but Allah's is the devising altogether. He knows what every soul earns. The unbelievers shall assuredly know whose will be the ultimate abode." This is saying, all deception/scheming is Allah's (*falillahi alp-makru* is the Arabic word). In fact, Allah raises wicked people to deceive and scheme for his purpose. Surah 6:123 states: "And even so We appointed in every city great ones among its sinners, to devise there; but they devised only against themselves, and they were not aware." Those verses indicate the purpose of these planted deceivers is to lead astray and then punish those who follow. What a contrast to the God of the Bible.

The Bible Says God Desires All to be Saved

In John 3:16-17 the Bible says: "For God so loved the world that He gave His only begotten Son, that whosoever believeth in him should not perish but have everlasting life. For God sent not his Son into the world to condemn the world, but that the world through him might be saved." Also in 1 Timothy 2:3-4, the Bible says: "For this is good and accept-able in the sight of God, our Savior, who will have all men to be saved, and to come unto the knowledge of the truth." What a contrast to Allah of the Quran.

God's desire is that all mankind come to a saving knowledge of the truth while Allah is scheming to lead mankind to hell.

Allah Punishes:

The perceived spiritual position a Muslim goes through must be agonizing. The god of their belief may lead them astray. Allah may have even risen up wicked people to help lead them into sin. Do the Muslims truly feel like their god could ambush them? The context is provided in the following Surahs:

1. Surah 78:21-30 (page 320):

> Behold, Gehenna has become an **ambush,** for the insolent a resort, therein to tarry for ages, tasting therein neither coolness nor any drink save boiling water and pus for a suitable recompense. They indeed hoped not for a reckoning, and they cried loud lies to Our signs; and everything We have numbered in a Book. Taste! We shall increase not save in chastisement.

2. Surah 35:6-7 (page 138): "Those who disbelieve- there awaits them a terrible chastisement; but those who believe, and do deeds of righteousness – theirs shall be forgiveness and a great wage."

Allah has prepared an ambush for the unbeliever. Allah leads astray whomever he desires through deceit, and then ambushes them with hell. No wonder Muhammad's head evangelist Abu Bakr was so distraught, fearing with even one foot in paradise he was still not safe. With the exception of martyrdom, a Muslim could get to the time of judgment thinking all is well and be ambushed by hell. This is not a god of love, but a god of vindictiveness. **In fact, the concept of godly love is neither presented or exemplified in the Quran!**

The God of the Bible Does Not Ambush
    The God of the Bible sets no ambush against man. In fact, He so loved the world that he came physically into this world and became the sacrifice for our sin. In Isaiah 9:6, we see **the person of this promise**; God in the person of Jesus Christ: "A child is born, a son is given, his name shall be called Wonderful, Counselor, **The Mighty God.**" In Philippians 2:5-8, we see the **provision of this promise**:

> Let this mind be in you, which was also in Christ Jesus. Who, being in the form of God, thought it not robbery to be equal with God, But made Himself of no reputation, and took upon Him the form of a servant, and was made in the likeness of men; And, being found in fashion as a man, He humbled himself and became obedient unto death, even the death of the cross.

In Isaiah 53:4-12 we see the **purpose of this promise**:

Surely he hath borne our griefs and carried our sorrows ... But He was wounded for our transgressions, He was bruised for our iniquities ... and the Lord hath laid on Him the iniquity of us all ... for the transgressions of my people was he stricken ... He had done no violence, **neither was any deceit in his mouth** ... He was numbered with the transgressors; and He bore the sin of many, and made intercession for the transgressors.

The God of the Bible provided the perfect plan for the redemption of mankind and neither used deceit or an ambush. Hell for those who reject the Savior of the Bible is a choice, not an ambush.

Allah's Reward:

Allah's reward focuses on the things that man experiences as they live life of earth. It is interesting Allah is proclaimed to be spirit. Yet, his rewards are physical in nature.

1. Surah 52:19-20 (page 241): "Surely god-fearing shall be in gardens and bliss, rejoicing in that the Lord has given them. Eat and drink with wholesome appetite for that your were working: reclining upon couches ranged in rows; and We shall espouse them to wide-eyed hours (Virgins)."

2. Surah 78:32 (page 321): Surely for the god-fearing a place of security gardens and vineyards and maidens with swelling breasts, like of age, and a cup overflowing.

Heaven or the reward in Paradise for a Muslim
is for the satisfaction of the *flesh*. Food, drink,
and sex are the reward. This is not the heaven
of the Bible. In Matthew 22:29-30 Jesus spoke
to the Sadducees who tried to trap Him. "Jesus
answered and said unto them, 'Ye do err, not
knowing the scriptures, nor the power of God.
For in the resurrection they neither marry, nor
are given in marriage, but are like the angels
of God in heaven.'"

Heaven is not an orgy to satisfy the flesh. In
Revelation 21:4, the Bible says: "And God shall
wipe away all tears from their eyes; and there shall
be no more death neither sorrow, nor crying, neither
shall there be any more pain; for the former things
are passed away."

Revelation 22:3 states: "And there shall be no
more curse, but the throne of God and of the Lamb
shall be in it, and his servants shall serve him." The
heaven of the Bible is about seeing and serving God,
not self-indulgence with women, wine, and song.

Allah Was a Familiar Name for Pagan Worshipers
(In the Pre-Islamic Assyria, Babylon and Arabia)
While researching the origin of the name Allah,
two scenarios surfaced. First was the name Allah,
which means god to Muhammad and the Muslim followers. No other significance is attached. Second, the
name has deep roots with the pre-Islamic culture of
Assyria, Babylon, Arabia, and even Israel. Sin was
the name of the moon god and his title was *al-ilah,*

"the deity" . The moon god Allah had several daughters—three of which are mentioned in the Quran as pagan; the forth was Ishtar. The moon god Sin was usually represented by the crescent moon in the crescent phase. [11] Following is a summary of the pre-Islamic religious culture:

1. Bel was the corresponding Babylonian god spoken of in Isaiah 46:1 and Jeremiah 50:2.

2. Mecca was built as a shrine for the moon god.

3. Allah was married to the Sun goddess the stars were their daughters. Some of their names were al-Lat, al-Uzza, Manat, and Ishtar. These are mentioned in Surah 53:20 (page 244): "Have you considered EL-Lat and EL-'Uzza and Manat the third, the other? What, have you males, and He females; that were indeed an unjust division. They are naught but names yourselves have named, and your fathers; Allah has sent down no authority touching them." Muhammad is denouncing the worship of the moon god daughters.

4. Moon god worship was the dominant pagan religion in Arabia. The Quraysh tribe of Mohammad was particularly devoted to Allah, the moon god, and especially to the three daughters of Sin.

5. Before Islam came into existence, the Sabbeans in Arabia worshipped the moon god Allah, who was married to the sun goddess.

---

[11] Editors of Encyclopedia Britannica "Sin Mesopotamian God", 2000.

6. Muhammad's father's name was Abd-Allah and his uncle's name was Obied-Allah.

7. Although the Islamic clerics are constantly saying that Allah is the only monotheist god of the Koran, "We" is constantly used in the creation narrative. Reference Surah 15: 1-25 (page 281-282). In this Surah, "WE" and "US" is used twenty times in these twenty-five verses. Further, "We" is used many times throughout the Quran speaking of the monotheist god Allah. To say Allah is one god and yet the Quran uses the plural "We" and "Us" is baffling. It is interesting that Muhammad attempts to bridge the gap between the pre-Islamic god Allah and YHVH, the God of the Bible. This mixture of paganism and worship of the true and living God is not new or unique. Today, it is called a cult.

8. The significance of the crescent moon with the pagan idol Allah (Sin, Bel) and its significance in modern day Islam:[12]

• Crescent moon engraved pagan idols abound in museums. Many pictures depict these stone idols with the crescent moon engraved on their chest.

• Crescent moon with Muslim country flags that depict the crescent moon include: Afghanistan, Libya, Pakistan, Algeria, Iran, Tunisia,

---

[12] Editors of Encyclopedia Britannica "Palmyra", last updated April 15,2016

Turkey, Malaysia, Tunisia, Turkmenistan, and Uzbekistan, to name some.

- Ramadan is the ninth month of the Islamic calendar. Starts with the new moon (crescent moon). Surah 2:179-184 (page 52) contains the instructions given by Allah to fast: "O believers, prescribed for you is the fast, even as it was prescribed for those that were before you – haply you will be god-fearing for days numbered … the month of Ramadan, wherein the Koran was sent down to be a guidance to the people, and as clear signs of the guidance and the salvation." Surah 2:185 (page 53): "They will question thee concerning the new moons. Say: 'They are appointed times for the people and the pilgrimage.'"

The **god Sin** and his daughter the **goddess Ishtar** were not alien to the Jews. The reference to **Ishtar,** the "Queen of Heaven," is found in Jeremiah Chapter 43 and 44. The context is: King Nebuchadnezzar, King of Babylon, had invaded Judah and destroyed Jerusalem. God determined this upon Judah because of their idolatry. Nebuchadnezzar had installed a ruler over the territory and Jewish zealots had assassinated him. Many of the Jews had fled to Egypt in fear of the retaliation by the Babylonians and had taken Jeremiah with them. Jeremiah warned these Jews that they would be destroyed because they continued to burn incense to other gods in the land of Egypt where they had gone (Jeremiah 44:8). There reply was they would not listen to Jeremiah and would continue to pour out drink offering to the queen of heaven. Jeremiah 44:18 best illustrates the Jews attitude toward Jeremiah and God: "But since we stopped burning incense to the queen of heaven and pouring out drink offerings to her, we have lacked everything and have been consumed by the sword and by famine." The Jews who had fled to Egypt continued their idolatrous practices and were destroyed as Jeremiah had prophesied.

The god Sin is not so obvious to the casual reader of the Bible, but was obvious to Nehemiah. After the seventy years of captivity that God had determined for the Jews to remain in captivity, Nehemiah, the cupbearer of King Artaxerxes, was allowed to return to Jerusalem to rebuild the city walls. There was great opposition to this effort coming from many. An opposing group who tried to thwart this effort was led by Sanballat, the Horonite. Nehemiah 4:1 states: "But it happened when Sanballat heard that we were rebuilding the wall, that he was furious and very indignant and mocked the Jews." The key to understanding the context is in the name Sanballat. It means "Sin has given life." The god Sin, the father of Ishtar, "Queen of heaven" was who this man was named after. Nehemiah knew what the name meant; he knew the history of the idolatry of the Jews in Jeremiah's day and wanted no part of Sanballat or his friends. The name Sanballat to Nehemiah would be equivalent to the name of a terrorist today whose first or middle name is Muhammad. To most, a terrorist attack by a person with a name including Muhammad is immediately associated with radical Islam. Nehemiah did not attempt to reconcile through dialogue or treaty, he knew what he dealt with. The Jews wanted no part of Allah—after the exile and return to Jerusalem, in Muhammad's day, and definitely not today.

Therefore, the question posed: Is Allah the god of Abraham or is Allah a carryover from the pagan god Sin, the moon god? Definitely **Allah of the Quran is not the God of the Bible!**

CHAPTER V
WHAT THE KORAN SAYS ABOUT JESUS CHRIST

When addressed in the Quran, the term Jesus Son of God is met with almost a demonic hatred, whereas the term "Jesus son of Mary" is accepted as only a messenger of Allah. To understand these differences, the birth, the concept of Jesus the Muslim messiah, and the deception at the crucifixion by Allah is presented. From the Hadith, the return of Jesus, son of Mary, his marriage, and future death and burial will be presented in Chapter XIII.

The following Surah verses provide the family origin of Mary, the announcement of the birth of Jesus to Mary, the birth of Jesus and the conflict that followed. Mary and Jesus are depicted as a sign from Allah and Jesus as a prophet of Allah.

Birth of Jesus: (The Surahs referenced are The House of Imran and Mary)
1. Surah 3:30-33 (page 77):

Allah chose Adam, Noah and the House of Abraham and the House of **Imran** above all beings, the seed of one another; Allah hears, and knows. When the wife of Imran said, "Lord, I have vowed to Thee, in dedication what is within my womb. Receive Thou this from me; thou hearest, and knowest." And when she gave birth to her she said, "Lord, I have given birth to her, a female." (And Allah knew very well what she had given birth to; the male is not as the female.) "And I have named her Mary, and commend her to Thee with her seed, to protect them from the accursed Satan."

2. Surah 3:30 (page 79): "When the angel said, 'Mary, Allah gives thee good tidings of a Word from Him whose name is Messiah. Jesus, son of Mary; high honored shall he be in this world and the next, near stationed to Allah. He shall speak to men in the cradle, and of age, and righteous he shall he be.'"

3. Surah 19:16-25 (page 331-332)

And mention in the Book Mary when she withdrew from her people to an eastern place, and she took a veil apart from them; then WE sent unto her OUR Spirit that presented himself to her a man without fault. She said, "I take refuge in the All-merciful from thee! If thou fearest Allah..." He said, "I am but a messenger come from thy Lord, to give thee a boy most pure." She said, "How shall I have a son whom no mortal has touched, neither have I been unchaste?" He said, "Even so thy Lord has said: 'Easy is that for ME; and that WE may appoint him a sign unto men and a mercy from US; it is a thing decreed.'" She conceived him, and withdrew with him to a distant place. And the birth pangs surprised her by the trunk of the palm-tree. She said, "Would I had died ere this, and become a thing forgotten!" But the one that was below her called to her, "Nay, do not sorrow; see thy Lord has set below thee a rivulet. Shake also to thee the palm-trunk and there shall come tumbling upon thee dates fresh and ripe. Eat therefore, and drink, and be comforted; and if thou shouldst see any mortal, say, 'I have vowed to the All-merciful a fast, and today I will not speak to any man.'"

4.   Surah 19:26-30 (page 332-333):

Then she brought the child to her folk carrying him; and they said, "Mary, thou hast surely committed a monstrous thing! **Sister of Aaron**, thy father was not a wicked man, nor was thy mother a woman unchaste." Mary pointed to the child then; but they said, "How shall we speak to one who is still in the cradle, a little child?" He said, "Lo, I am Allah's servant; Allah has given me the Book, and made me a Prophet."

5. Surah 23:51 (page 40): "We made Mary's son,
    and his mother, to be a sign, and gave them
    refuge upon a height, where was a hollow and
    a spring."

With each Surah from the Quran stated above,
a comparison of the content is made with the Bible.
First is the announcement of the birth of Mary. In
Luke 3:23-38, the genealogy of Mary is given going
through King David and the tribe of Judah not the
tribe of Levi of which Aaron was from. Second, In
Exodus 6:20, the father of Moses, Aaron, and Miriam
was Amram. There is no mention in the Bible of any
family of Imran. Third, the book of Exodus was
written by Moses approximately 1450 BC and the
Gospels giving the background of Mary written in
AD 50. A 1500-year error in the Quran. It looks like
Muhammad got confused when stating Mary was the
sister of Aaron. It is Miriam who was the sister of
Aaron. If you research this, you see an attempt by
Muslims to explain it away.

The second and third referenced Surah verses
announce the birth of Jesus. Surah 3:30 indicates an
angel made the announcement where Surah 19:16-25
indicates the spirit of Allah in a man without fault
made the announcement. Two problems surface here.
Was it an angel or was it a man? If Allah were only
spirit, how would he indwell a man without fault to
deliver the message? The Quran constantly flips back
and forth from Allah is one to the use of We, and Us.
Here it looks like Allah takes on the person of a man

through his spirit. Surah 19 in its context would challenge the idea that Allah is only spirit.

Surah 19 also provides the event of the birth of Jesus. The birth occurred under a date palm tree not in Bethlehem in a manger. Mary was alone and instructed not to speak to any man, indicating Joseph was not there. In fact, Joseph, the husband of Mary, is not mentioned in the Quran. There is no reference to Mary ever marrying after the birth of Jesus and obviously, no mention of her having any other children. For relief of birth pangs during the labor process, Mary is instructed to shake the tree and eat some dates for comfort. This whole scenario in no way represents what happened in the four gospels.

Surah 3 and Surah 19 indicate Jesus would and did speak as an infant in the cradle to adults. The ability of the baby Jesus to defend Mary as she was accused by her family as being promiscuous is found nowhere in the prophesies or the gospels of the Bible.

Jesus, the Muslim Messiah:

One of the most recurring themes in the Quran is: Jesus is the son of Mary, not the Son of God. Jesus in the Quran in no way resembles Jesus in the Bible. The Jesus of the Quran was only a messenger of Allah, created by Allah, not the Creator. The Jesus of the Quran did perform miracles. The Quran states in Surah 3:40-44 and Surah 5:110-12 that Jesus could speak to men in the cradle, he created a bird out of clay and breathed life into it and healed the blind, the leper, and raised some from the dead. Surah 5 states:

When Allah said, "Jesus Son of Mary, remember My blessing upon thee and upon thy mother, when I confirmed thee with the Holy Spirit, to speak to men in the cradle, and of age; and when I taught thee the Book, the Wisdom, the Torah, the Gospel; and when thou createst out of clay, by My leave, as the likeness of a bird, and thou breathiest into it, and it is a bird, by My leave; and thou healest the blind and the leper by My leave, and thou bringest the dead forth by my leave..."

With the exception of Jesus speaking from the cradle and creating a bird, the miracles of healing and raising Lazarus from the dead are recorded in the Gospels. However, so many times a reference to the Bible will have some bit of consistency followed by something else that is totally alien.

Opposition to Jesus being the Son of God is put forth in the argument that this would be two gods. If two gods existed, then Allah the greatest would be dominant over any other. Further stated is Jesus Himself when questioned by Allah concerning he and his mother Mary being gods, denies his own deity. Of course this is completely inconsistent with the Bible. The following Surah verses validates these positions:

1. Surah 5:19 (page 130): "They are unbelievers who say,' God is the Messiah, Mary's son.' Say: 'Who then shall overrule Allah in any way if Allah desires to destroy the Messiah, Mary's son, and his mother, and all those who are on earth?'"

2. Surah 5:76-77, 79 (page 139): "They are unbelievers who say, 'God is the Messiah, Mary's son.' For the Messiah said, 'Children of Israel, serve Allah, my lord and your Lord. Verily whoso associates with Allah anything, Allah shall prohibit him entrance to Paradise and his refuge shall be Fire; and wrongdoers shall have no helpers.'"

77: "They are unbelievers who say, 'Allah is the Third of Three.' No god is there but One Allah."
79: "The Messiah, Son of Mary was only a Messenger."

3. Surah 5:115: "And when Allah said, 'O Jesus son of Mary,' didst thou say unto men, 'Take me and my mother as gods, apart from Allah'? He said, 'To Thee be glory! It is not mine to say what I have no right to. I only said to them what Thou didst command me: "serve Allah, my Lord and your Lord."'"

4. Surah 6:101 (page 161): "The creator of the heavens and the earth – how should he have a son, seeing that he has no consort, and he created all things, and he has knowledge of everything?"

5. Surah 23:92 (page 43): "Allah has not taken to himself any son, nor is there any god with him; for then each god would have taken off that he created and some of them would have risen up over others; glory to Allah."

These Surahs emphasize two things: there is no denial that Jesus is the Messiah. However, what is made clear is Jesus is not deity, not the Son of God, not God in the flesh. The Quran equates Jesus to no more than one of the messengers sent by Allah and less than Muhammad. The Bible speaks clearly as to who is the Messiah. Again, in Isaiah 9:6: "For unto us a child is born, unto us a son is given, and the government shall be upon his shoulder; and his name shall be called Wonderful, Counselor, The Mighty God, The Everlasting Father, the Prince of Peace." Birth to mighty God is absolute. Again, how can Muslim scholars attempt to use the book of Isaiah to validate Muhammad as the seal of the prophets and totally ignore Isaiah 9:6 and the whole chapter of Isaiah 53?

Jesus Not Crucified:

The Bible presents the crucifixion of Jesus Christ in all four gospels. Even the Jewish historian Flavius Josephus records the crucifixion in volume IV of the Antiquities of the Jews Book XVIII[13]. Josephus is one of the most recognized historians of the apostolic age. He was born in AD 37 or 38 and had firsthand knowledge of the turmoil in Jesus' day and the destruction of Jerusalem in AD 70 by the Roman General Titus. He was not a Christian. He was a Pharisee. However, the Quran denies the crucifixion of Jesus and makes limited mention of the miracles Jesus performed and His teachings. In fact, the teachings of Jesus according to

---

[13] Willian Whiston trans, "The Works of Flavius Josephus" Reprinted 1974.

the Bible are not mentioned. These two references to the crucifixion put forth the Muslim belief:

1. Surah 4:155 (page 123): "We slew the Messiah, Jesus Son of Mary, the messenger of Allah." Yet they did not slay him, neither crucified him only a likeness of that was shown to them. Those who are at variance concerning him surely are in doubt regarding him, they have no knowledge of him, except the following of surmise, and they slew him not of a certainty – no indeed.

2. Surah 4:169 (page 125): "People of the Book (Bible), go not beyond the bounds in your religion, and say not as to Allah but the truth. The Messiah, Jesus son of Mary, was only the messenger of Allah, and his word that he committed to Mary, and a Spirit from Him. So, believe in Allah and his messengers, and say not 'Three: Refrain; better it is for you.'"

These two Surah verses not only deny the deity of Jesus, but refute the Holy Spirit. Further, they indicate Allah tricked and deceived all who witnessed the crucifixion of Jesus, indicating it was only a likeness of Jesus who was crucified.

Arguments By Muslims Using the Bible to Say Jesus is Not God.

(Source: The Institute of Islamic Information and Education- distributed at Purdue University, March 2006.)

1. Allah is all knowing, but Jesus was not:

Matthew 24:36: "But of that day and hour no man knows, not even the Angels in heaven but my father only."

Many of these types of statements go unchallenged by Christians because of the lack of understanding of the God of the Bible coming in the flesh, Jesus the Son of God. What does the Bible say concerning the restriction of conveying knowledge from Jesus to His disciples? Isaiah 9:6 again gives the order of a child is born to being the Mighty God, the Everlasting Father. John 1:1-2 and 14 states: "In the beginning was the Word and the Word was with God, and the **Word was God.** The same was in the beginning with God. And the **Word was made flesh,** and dwelt among us (and we beheld his glory, the glory as of the only begotten of the Father), full of grace and truth." Also, in Philippians 2:5-8, we see the state in which God in the flesh came to serve and save:

Let this mind be in you, which was also in Christ Jesus, Who being in the form of God, thought it not robbery to be equal with God. But made himself of no reputation, and took upon him the form of a servant, and was made in the likeness of men; And, being found in fashion as a man, he humbled himself and became obedient unto death even the death of the cross.

A lot will take place between the time of a child is born to Mighty God and Everlasting Father when Father, Son, and Holy Spirit is All in All (1 Corinthians 15:28). To understand what Jesus said to His disciples in Matthew 24:36 is to first look at the context of God emptying Himself, humbling Himself and coming to this earth in the form of man. In so doing, God purposely restricted Himself while here on earth in many ways. When He told His disciples that He must go before the Holy Spirit would come is because Jesus restricted Himself in teaching physically and orally; where the Holy Spirit (the Spirit of Jesus, Son of God) would indwell mankind to teach them many things that they could not understand at that time (John 16:12-15). That restriction was removed after the resurrection. Luke 24:45 states: "Then opened he their understanding, that they might understand the scriptures."

A second part of that restriction resides in the Word was made flesh. The Word of God said when the second coming will occur had not been spoken. At the time of Jesus Christ coming to earth as the suffering servant, the second coming of Jesus had not been foreordained. If not foreordained at that time, then there would not have been a need for foreknowledge. Therefore, it was not part of the Word made flesh as Jesus offered himself as the redeemer of humanity.

In some cases, God provides specific times; in others, He does not. This should not come as a surprise. In Daniel 9:2 and Jeremiah 25:11, God tells the prophets, "Judah will remain in captivity for seventy years." The seventy years of captivity for Judah was foreordained, thus the foreknowledge of God was revealed. However, in Daniel 9:21-27, we see specific time periods mentioned such as from the rebuilding of Jerusalem to the coming of Messiah, and the tribulation period, yet the gap between the sixty-ninth and seventieth week (Weeks of Years), the Church Age, is not given. Many references of the Bible would indicate God had not at that time preordained that time period.

As the Bible has been used in context to explain the Muslim spin on Jesus not being all-knowing, the Quran will be used in context to show Allah is not all-knowing. Allah, according to the Quran, is reactive and must use (*makara*) scheming, deception, lying, double-dealing, and double-crossing to accomplish his purpose. Why is this? Because he cannot foreordain or predestinate an event; therefore, he has no foreknowledge (Surah 3:46; 7:99,181; 8:30). However, Jesus most assuredly had foreknowledge. Here are just a few examples: Jesus told the disciples that Jerusalem would be destroyed and not one stone of the temple would remain on top of the other. Jesus told His disciples He would be betrayed and would be crucified; Jesus told Peter he would deny Him. Jesus knew Lazarus was dead and purposely waited three days before going to raise him. Most importantly, Jesus told His disciples He would die on the cross and be resurrected.

2. **Allah is all-powerful but Jesus was not**: John 5:19: "Most assuredly, I say to you the Son of Man can do nothing of Himself but what he seeth the Father do; for whatever things he doeth, these also doeth the Son in the same manner."

The context of Jesus was not all-powerful presupposes the Father, Son, and Holy Spirit act separately when they do not. They are in complete unity because they are one. Jesus was all-powerful, but within the plan and purpose of the Trinity. Jesus, God in the flesh, would never do anything to counter the all-in-all purpose.

When the Quran states Allah is all-powerful, there appears to be a contradiction. Why would Allah have to make a binding deal of Paradise with Muslims to fight and die for him to accomplish his purpose? The God of the Bible needs not and does not configure that sort of deal because He is truly all-powerful.

3. **Allah does not have a god, but Jesus did**: John 20:17: "I ascend to my Father and your Father and to my God and your God." (By the way: this was after the crucifixion and resurrection of Jesus, which the Quran says did not happen; using a source you don't believe in to prove something you do believe in is baffling.)

When man speaks of himself, he speaks many times of the body (flesh: my arm, my leg). Other times, people speak of thoughts, feelings, and actions according to those thoughts and feelings. A depiction of one's character, and that which distinguishes them from someone else, even an identical twin. This is defined as one's soul. Then one may speak in terms of the spirit ("the spirit moved me") that which cannot be humanly defined. Mankind is in fact a trinity (body, soul, spirit). The flesh (body) looks to the thoughts, feelings, and perceptions for direction. One does not operate without the other; yet they are one human being. Genesis 1:26-27 states "And God said, 'Let us make man in our image, after our likeness' ... So God created man in his own image, in the image of God created he him; male and female created he them." We can understand much about the God of the Bible by looking at ourselves. God is a trinity just as man in God's image is a trinity. As man's body looks to the mind and soul of man, so does God in the flesh (Jesus) looks to the Father.

4. **Allah is an invisible spirit, but Jesus was flesh and blood**: John 4:24: "God is a spirit and they that worship him must worship him in spirit and truth."

What Jesus said to the adulterous Samaritan woman was all mankind must worship God in spirit and truth. First, one cannot be spiritually dead and worship God. Ephesians 2:1 states: "And you hath he made alive who were dead in trespasses and sins," and Ephesians 2:5-6 says, "Even when we were dead in sins, hath made us alive together with Christ (for by grace ye are saved), and hath raised us up together and made us sit together in heavenly places in Christ Jesus."

Second, the woman needed to be saved; she was spiritually dead and the Savior stood before her. Jesus said in John 14:6: "I am the way, the truth, and the life; no man cometh unto the Father but by me." To worship God, we must be spiritually alive and then we can truly worship. Further, it was only after the resurrection of Jesus by his Spirit did the disciples realize He was truly God the Son. When Thomas realized who the risen Lord was in John 20:28, he worshiped Jesus: "And Thomas answered, and said unto him, 'My Lord and My God.'" When Jesus ascended into heaven, Luke recorded the event in Luke 24:51-53 "And he led them out as far as to Bethany; and he lifted up his hands. And blessed them. And it came to pass, while he blessed them, He was parted from them, and carried up into heaven. **And they worshiped him** and returned to Jerusalem with great joy."

To further counter, the out of context argument, the statement: "Allah is an invisible Spirit but Jesus was flesh and blood" is a poor approach. In fact, using Surah 19:16-25, we find Allah sent his spirit in the form of a man to speak to Mary: "then We sent unto her Our Spirit that presented himself to her a man without fault. She said, 'I take refuge in the all-merciful from thee! If thou fearest Allah...' He said, 'I am but a messenger come from thy Lord, to give thee a boy most pure.'" Allah continues to get caught in a catch twenty-two by the Quran regarding him being spirit and flesh.

The internet and social media is full of attempts by Muslim pundits and scholars trying to use the Bible as a tool to recruit. The written arguments are weak, out of context, but could be persuasive to a religious novice who knows little about the Bible. Christians cannot remain ignorant of what is going on. What you do not know will hurt you as well as others.

What the Bible says in a few verses that the Quran does not say and the Muslims will not acknowledge:

1. Isaiah 9:6: "For unto us a child is born, unto us a son is given, and the government shall be upon his shoulder; and his name shall be called Wonderful, Counselor, **The Mighty God**, the Everlasting Father, the Prince of Peace."

2. John 14:6: "Jesus saith unto him, 'I am the way, the truth and the life, no man cometh unto the Father but by me.'"

3. John 1:1: "In the beginning was the Word and the Word was with God and the Word was God."

4. John 1:14: "And the Word was made flesh and dwelt among us (and we beheld his glory, the glory as of the only begotten of the father), full of grace and truth."

5. John 10:30: "I and my Father are one."

6. John 17:22: (Part of Christ's prayer for the believer) "And the glory which thou gavest me I have given them that they may be one, even as we are one."

7. Luke 22:70-71: "Then they all said, 'Are you then the son of God?' So He (Jesus) said to them, 'You rightly say that I am.' And they said, 'What further testimony do we need? For we have heard it ourselves from his own mouth.'"

8. Acts 4:11-12: "The Apostle Peter addressed the Sanhedrin and the High Priest: 'This is the stone (Jesus) which was rejected by you builders which has become the chief corner stone. Nor is there salvation in any other for there is no other name under heaven given among men by which we must be saved.'"

These Bible verses from both the Old and New Testaments present emphatically God coming in the flesh, in the person of God the Son. Unlike the Quran, in the Bible, Jesus does not deny his deity, but states He and the Father are one. Even when being interrogated by the Chief Priests prior to being crucified, Jesus proclaims his deity. The proclamation in Luke 22:70 seals his commitment to go to the cross. The Bible plainly states salvation is only in and through Jesus Christ. There is no other way. From Genesis through Revelation, the plan of salvation is presented. There is no other name under heaven given among men by which we must be saved. Not the Quran, not Allah, not Muhammad—Jesus and Jesus alone. **What a contrast in doctrine!**

CHAPTER VI
WHAT THE QURAN SAYS ABOUT THE HOLY SPIRIT AND THE TRINITY

The Holy Spirit and the Trinity in the Quran

Muhammad's view of the Holy Spirit was different from the Spirit of YHVH in the Old and New Testament. The Holy Spirit is not depicted as the Spirit of Allah, but a Holy Spirit involved in the announcement of the birth of Jesus, the confirmation of who Jesus, Son of Mary was and the confirmation of the Quran to be the truth from Allah. The following Surah verses illustrate this:

1. Surah 2:254 (page 64): "And We gave Jesus Son of Mary the clear signs and confirmed him with the Holy Spirit."
2. Surah 19:16-17 (page 331): "And mention in the Book Mary when she withdrew from her people to an eastern place, and she took

a veil apart from them; then We sent unto her Our Spirit that presented himself to her a man without fault."

3. Surah 5:110 (page 145): "When Allah said, 'Jesus Son of Mary, remember my blessing upon thee and upon thy mother when I confirmed thee with the Holy Spirit.'"

4. Surah 16:104 (page 298): "Say: 'The Holy Spirit sent it (Quran) down from thy Lord in truth, and to confirm those who believe, and to be a guidance and good tidings to those who surrender.'"

5. Surah 5:77-78 (page 140): "They are unbelievers who say, 'Allah is the Third of Three.' No god is there but One Allah."

6. Surah 97:1-5: "The night of power sent down in it the angels and the Spirit descend."

Although Muhammad speaks of a Holy Spirit, including Allah (We) sending his spirit in the form of a man without fault to announce to Mary the birth of Jesus (Surah 19:16-17), he denies the Holy spirit being any part of the godhead. The position is clearly stated in Surah 5:77: they are unbelievers who say, "Allah is the Third of Three. No god is there but one Allah". **Further, Muhammad's adamant opposition to Jesus the Son of God coming in the flesh, according to the Bible, is confusing when considering his position on Allah presenting himself in the flesh to Mary through his spirit.** Muhammad clearly denies the trinity as revealed in the Bible. He is emphatic that acknowledging the trinity is the same as worshiping three gods.

Again, there appears to be confusion. In the Holy Bible, it is understood by Christians that God is *one* with three personalities: Father, Son, and Holy Spirit. In the Quran, Allah is one god; there is a Holy Spirit; it is not an angel, not a Jinn, not defined. Also, "we" and "us" are used many times in the description of the creation (Surah 15:1-25, page 282) as well as other Surahs. The deity of Jesus Christ is clearly denied; no explanation of the Holy Spirit is provided. Allah is one personality yet "We" is used over and over in the Surahs.

A Muslim study group member from Turkey demonstrated either confusion or ignorance of the Quran while I was in graduate school. While discussing with another member of the study group concerning his recent salvation experience and acceptance of Jesus Christ as Lord and Savior, the Muslim lady stated: "My mother told me Allah could not come in the flesh; he is not flesh. At that time, I did not understand the basis for the statement, but neither did she."

The Holy Spirit and the Trinity in the Bible

The Bible clearly teaches God in three persons from Genesis to Revelation. In Genesis 1:1-2, the Scripture says: "In the beginning God created the heaven and the earth. And the earth was without form, and void; and darkness was upon the face of the deep. And the **Spirit of God** moved upon the face of the waters." There is no question this is two persons of the godhead; Father and Holy Spirit. God the Son is made evident in the Garden of Eden when the pre-incarnate Jesus Christ questions Adam and Eve for eating the fruit from the forbidden tree (Genesis 3:8-13).

Again, God in the flesh visits Abraham and Sarah announcing the birth of Isaac and the destruction of Sodom (Genesis 18:1-22). "And the Lord appeared unto him (Abraham) by the oaks of Mamre: and he sat in the tent door in the heat of the day. And he lifted up his eyes and looked, and lo, three men stood by him" (Verse 1, 2A). "And the men turned their faces from there and went toward Sodom: but Abraham stood yet before the Lord" (Verse 22).

Moses learned man couldn't behold the face of the Heavenly Father. In Exodus 33:18-23, Moses petitioned God the Father to see His glory. God said to Moses in Verse 20: "And he said, thou canst not see my face for there shall no man see me, and live." When God questioned Adam and Eve, it was the Son of God. When Abraham spoke face to face with God, it was God the Son. When Joshua met the Captain of the Lord's host when Israel was about to conquer Jericho, again it was God in the flesh. Joshua 5:14-15 says:

And he said, "Nay, but the captain of the host of the Lord am I now come." And Joshua fell on his face to the earth, and did worship and said unto him, "What saith my lord unto his servant?" And the captain of the Lord's host said unto Joshua, Loose thy shoe from off thy foot; for the place whereon thou standest is holy and Joshua did so.

Joshua could not have met and spoke to God the Father face to face. Joshua did not speak to a spirit. Joshua spoke to God the Son, a picture of God the Son as he will come in Revelation 19:11-16, conquering King of Kings and Lord of Lords.

The Quran portrays Allah in many of the Surah verses as omnipotent, all-hearing, all-wise, all-knowing, all-seeing, all-high, all-great, all-powerful, all-aware, all-subtitle, all-pardoning, all-compassionate, all-merciful, all-glorious, and all-mighty. Muhammad uses these terms over and over to describe Allah. These can be compared to the attributes of the God of the Bible: omnipotent (all-powerful), omnipresent (all-present) and omniscient (all-knowing). If the supreme being of the universe has these attributes, could these simple questions be answered?

1. If the God of creation is omnipotent, omniscient, and omnipresent, is it possible for Him to be in His Spirit in more than one place at one time? Yes!

2. If the God of creation is omnipotent, omniscient, and omnipresent, is it possible for Him to indwell flesh? Yes!

3. If the God of creation is omnipotent, omniscient, and omnipresent, is it possible for Him to condemn and judge sin, be the recipient of that judgment, and lead mankind through the teaching of His Holy Spirit to that discerning knowledge? Yes!

Jesus told His disciples in John 15:26: "But when the Comforter is come, whom I will send unto you from the Father, Even the Spirit of truth (Holy Spirit), who proceedeth from the Father, he shall testify of me:" Again, in John 16:7, Jesus said, "Nevertheless, I tell you the truth: It is expedient for you that I go away; for if I go not away, the Comforter will not come unto you; but if I depart, I will send him unto you." **Why would the Holy Spirit not come until Jesus departed from this world?** At that time, God had restricted Himself in the flesh as He appeared to mankind. The teachings to the disciples came directly through Jesus in a visible, audible, undeniable manner. They were limited in learning because of their own flesh. When God the Son ascended back into heaven, His Holy Spirit (there is no difference in the Holy Spirit and the Spirit of the Lord Jesus Christ) was free to indwell the disciples to teach them. Jesus said in John 16:12-14:

> I have many things to say unto you, but ye cannot bear them now. Nevertheless, when he, the Spirit of truth, is come, he will guide you into all truth; for he shall not speak of himself, but whatever he shall hear, that shall he speak; and he will show you things to come. He shall glorify me; for he shall receive of mine, and shall show it unto you.

After the ascension, the Holy Spirit was poured out upon the Church at Pentecost. Acts 2:4 records this event: "And they were all filled with the Holy Spirit and began to speak with other tongues, as the Spirit gave them utterance." God's power was manifested through His Spirit to the church to do great things!

The Trinity of God from the beginning to the end of Time

To understand the work of the Trinity from the beginning to the end of time is to understand the consequences of sin. In the beginning, at the time of the creation, God was all in all as Father, Son, and Holy Spirit. When sin came into the world through Adam, it separated mankind from God. Man could only behold God in the flesh, not in God's full glory lest man die. God revealed this to Moses. God in the person of the pre-incarnate Christ (in the flesh) revealed himself to Abraham and to Joshua. God in the person of the Holy Spirit came upon Gideon (Judges 6:34), Zechariah (2 Chronicles 24:20), Saul (1 Samuel 10:10), David (1 Samuel 23:2), Azariah (2 Chronicles 15:1), and Ezekiel (Ezekiel 11:5). The incarnate Christ walked on the face of the earth teaching His disciples about the coming of the Kingdom of God. The Holy Spirit was restrained at this time as Jesus indicated in John 16:12-14. Upon the ascension of Jesus Christ into heaven after His resurrection, the Holy Spirit was no longer restrained. The Holy Spirit was again prominent at Pentecost establishing the early church. The Holy Spirit is now prominent among believers giving spiritual gifts to edify the church (1 Corinthians 12:1-4) while reproving the world of sin and of righteousness and of judgment (John 16:8).

The work of the Holy Spirit will again be restrained when the church is raptured (1 Thessalonians 4:16). This is when the church is caught up together with him (Jesus) in the clouds to meet the Lord in the air, and so shall we ever be with the Lord (1 Thessalonians 4:17). This will last through the tribulation period and the 1000-year reign of the incarnate Lord Jesus Christ. At the end of the 1000-year reign of the Lord Jesus Christ, death and hell will be cast into the lake of fire. At this time God, will again be all in all.

God All in All

So, what is meant by God being "all in all" and how will man one day see and understand the trinity of God? Paul speaks to this in a letter to the Corinthians. In 1 Corinthians 15, Paul is speaking to the importance of the resurrection and the completeness of the godhead. Starting with verse 24 of chapter 15:

> **Then cometh the end**, when he shall have delivered up the kingdom to God, even the father, when he shall have put down all rule and all authority and power, for he must reign, till he hath put all enemies under his feet. The last enemy that shall be destroyed is death. For he hath put all things under his feet. But when he saith all things are put under him, it is manifest that he is excepted who did put all things under him. And when all things shall be subdued unto him, then shall the Son also himself be subject unto him that put all things under him **that God may be all in all.**

When death and Hades are cast into the lake of fire (Revelation 20:14), the last enemy is destroyed. The new heaven and earth will be the dwelling place of Christians with the all in all godhead.

CHAPTER VII
WHO IS SATAN AND
WHAT COMPRISES THE
SPIRITUAL WORLD?

According to the Quran, the spiritual world is made of angels and Jinn. The use of the following verses from the Quran provides for the foundation for what Muhammad believed:

Angels Depicted in the Quran:
1. Surah 2:33 (page 33): "We said to the angels, 'Bow yourselves to Adam' so they bowed themselves save Iblis, he refused and waxed proud and so became one of the unbelievers."
2. Surah 2:92 (page 40): "Whosoever is an enemy to Allah and his angels and his messengers, and Gabriel and Michal surely Allah is an enemy to the unbelievers."
3. Surah 35:2 (page 138): "Allah appointed the angels to be messengers."

4. Surah 66:6 (page 288): "Believers, guard yourselves and your families against a fire whose fuel is men and stones and over which harsh, terrible angels who disobey not Allah in what he commends them and do what they are commanded."

5. Surah 66:4 (page 287): "Allah is his (Muhammad's) protector, and Gabriel, and the righteous among the believers; and, after that, the angels are his supporters."

6. Surah 3:120 (page 89): "Yea; if you are patent and god-fearing, and the foe come against you instantly, your Lord will reinforce you with five thousand swooping angels."

7. Surah 2:285 (page 71): "The Messenger believes in what was sent down to him from his Lord, and the believers; each one believes in Allah and His angels. And in His Books and His Messengers."

8. Surah 4:164 (page 124): "But Allah bears witness to that He has sent down to thee; He has sent it down with His knowledge; and the angels also bear witness; and Allah suffices for a witness."

9. Surah 16:3 (page 287): "High be he exalted above that they associate with Him! He sends down the angels with the Spirit of His command upon whomsoever He will among His servants, saying: Give you warning that there is no god but Allah; so fear Me!"

Angels' Position and Duties

By being required to bow to Adam, angels are portrayed as being subservient in position to man—especially Muhammad. Although Muhammad claimed Gabriel delivered the Quran to him from Allah as he retreated to a cave for prayer, Gabriel is assigned to protect Muhammad and messengers in general. They are also dispatched to fight for the Muslim.

Angels have the duty of bearing witness to the Quran and that Allah is one implying there is no trinity. Surah 74:30 (page 311) states: "We have appointed only angels to be masters of the fire." So, not only were angels required to protect and support the prophets and messengers, they also had the duty of overseeing hell where unbelievers will go to be severely punished. Surah 78:25 (page 320) states: "Behold, Gehenna has become an ambush, for the insolent a resort, therein to tarry for ages, tasting therein neither coolness nor any drink save boiling water and pus for a suitable recompense." This would indicate as the angels have oversight over Gehenna (hell), they would provide the pus and boiling water to the unbeliever to drink.

Jinn are the Second Spiritual Group Muhammad Portrays in the Quran.

According to early Arabian and later Islamic mythology and theology, Jinn are supernatural creatures created by Allah from smokeless fire, but are physical in nature. The Jinn can interact with people and objects and can be acted upon. Like human beings, the Jinn can be good, evil, or neutrally benevolent and therefore have a free will like human beings and will be judged at the resurrection.

Archeological evidence found in Northwestern Arabia appears to indicate the worship of Jinn hundreds of years before Islam. Numerous mentions of Jinn in the Quran and testimony of both pre-Islamic and Islamic literature indicate the belief in spirits was prominent among the pre-Islamic Bedouin. Following are some of the Surah verses describing the nature and activity of Jinn:

1. **Satan was a Jinn**: Surah 2:32-34 (page 33) says:

> And when We said to the angels, "Bow yourselves to Adam;" so they bowed themselves, save Iblis; he refused, and waxed proud, and so he became one of the unbelievers. And We said, "Adam, dwell thou, and thy wife, in the Garden, and eat thereof easefully where you desire; but draw not nigh the tree, lest you be evildoers." Then Satan caused them to slip there from and brought them out of that they were in.

Here Satan is identified as Iblis, but Iblis was not an angel. He was a Jinn. In Surah 18:46 (page 322), Muhammad makes it clear: "And when We said to the angels, 'Bow yourselves to Adam;' so, they bowed themselves save **Iblis, he was one of the Jinn.**"

2. **Creation of Jinn in the Quran**: Surah 55:14 (page 251): "He created man of clay like the

potter's and he created the Jinn of a smokeless fire."

3. **Jinn interaction with man**: Surah 6:127
   (page 164):

On the day when he shall muster them all together
"company of Jinn, you have made much of mankind." Then their friends among mankind will say,
"Our lord we have profited each of the other, and we
have reached the term determined by thee for us." He
will say: "The fire is your lodging, therein to dwell
forever."

Here is a situation where both Jinn and mankind
have worked together on earth. During the final judgment, both believe they have done the will of Allah;
yet, they will be cast into hell.

4. **Jinn served Solomon**: Allah placed the Jinn
   as servants to Solomon for not obeying. They
   did not realize Solomon had died; he had
   died leaning on his staff. The Jinn continued
   to serve until a worm came out of the ground
   and ate Solomon's staff, causing Solomon's
   dead body to fall to the ground. At this point,
   the Jinn realized they did not have to continue
   to serve Solomon. This narrative is provided
   in Surah 34:11-14 (pages 132-133):

And to Solomon the wind; its morning course
was a month's journey, and its evening course
was a month's journey. And We made the
Fount of Molten Brass to flow for him. And
of the Jinn, some worked before him by the

leave of his Lord; and such of them as swerved away from Our commandment, We would let them taste the chastisement of the Blaze; fashioning for him whatsoever he would- places of worship, statues, porringers like water-troughs, and anchored cooking-pots. "Labour, O House of David, in thankfulness; for few indeed are those that are thankful among My servants." And when We decreed that he should die, (Solomon), naught indicated to them (the Jinn) that he was dead but the Beast (worm) of the Earth devouring his staff and when he fell down, the Jinn saw clearly that, had they only known the Unseen. They would not have continued in humbling chastisement.

5. Judgment of Jinn: Surah 6:130:

"Company of Jinn and mankind, did not Messengers come to you from among you, relating to you My signs and warning you of the encounter of this your day?" They shall say, "We bear witness against ourselves." They were deluded by the present life, and they, bear witness against themselves that **they were unbelievers.**

Surah 72:1-2 (page 305) is titled "The Jinn." "Say: 'It has been revealed to me that a company of the Jinn gave ear,' then they said, 'We have indeed heard a Koran wonderful guiding to rectitude. We believe in it and we will not associate with our Lord anyone.'"

Surah 72:11: "And some of us are the righteous, and some of us are otherwise; we are sects differing."

Surah 72:14-15: "And some of us have surrendered, and some of us have deviated, those who have surrendered sought rectitude; but as for those who have deviated, they have become firewood for Gehenna!" Two different groups of Jinn are depicted. One group is "bad" because they saw the signs from Allah, but were deluded by the ways of the world and will therefore be sent to hell. The second group of Jinn heeded the Koran, did not associate Jesus, the Holy Spirit, or anyone with Allah and therefore are allowed to enter paradise.

Angels Superior to Jinn

The Quran depicts Angels to be of a higher order than Jinn. First, Jinn are required to serve man physically. Such service is indicated as Solomon was served by Jinn. Second, according Surah 6:130, Jinn will be judged at the resurrection; angels will not be judged. According Ibrahim B. Syed in his book, *The Muslim Belief in Angels,* Islamic theology presents angels as not having free will and therefore cannot sin. They are completely obedient and closer to Allah. Third, Angels are required to support the prophets and messengers, not serve them. Fourth, angels are depicted in the Quran to have greater power than their Jinn counterpart.

A major implication of the hierarchy is the power of Satan in the Quran. Satan is a Jinn according to Surah 18:46. Therefore, he is not as powerful as the angels. This would be completely contrary to the Bible where we see Satan more powerful than angels and as powerful as the archangels. Satan in the Bible is on a different level than that of the Satan of the Quran.

What the Bible Says About Satan

In the Quran, Iblis' (Satan's) fall was due to his disobedience in not bowing to Adam. First, the Bible accounts no such incident and second, there is no mention of Jinn anywhere in the Bible. In Isaiah 14:13-14, the Scripture states how Lucifer (Satan) is fallen from heaven, how he is cut down to the ground because he has said in his heart he would exalt his throne above the stars of God and be like the most high God. Lucifer (Satan) falls because of pride and rebellion against God. Satan's characteristics are: He is **wicked** according to 1 John 2:13; He is **subtle** according to 2 Corinthians 11:13; He is **deceitful** according to Ephesians 6:11; He is **cruel** according to 1 Peter 5:8 and He is a **liar** and a **murderer** according to John 8:44; Satan **hinders the gospel** (Matthew 13:19) and **blinds the minds** of them who do not believe in Jesus Christ, the Son of God (2 Corinthians 4:4). God prepared hell for Satan and his angels because of their rebellion and wickedness (Matthew 25:41). Satan still has access to the throne of God as the accuser of Christians (Job 1:9, 2:4), but will one day be contained here on earth during the tribulation period. Revelation 12:12 states, "Woe to the inhibiters of the earth and the sea! For the devil is come down unto you, having great wrath, because he knoweth that he hath but a short time." Once the tribulation period begins, Satan knows how much time he has before he will be cast into hell. At the end of the seven years of tribulation, Satan will be bound in the abyss during the Kingdom age, released after a thousand years to tempt the nations, defeated, and then cast into hell for eternity (Revelation 20:1-10).

Considering the biblical characteristics of Satan (subtle, deceitful, cruel, liar, murderer), he has more in common with Muhammad and Allah of the Quran than Allah has in common with the God of the Bible.

What the Bible Says About Fallen Angels and Demons

Satan leads a host of fallen angels and demons that go about doing his bidding. Many students of the Bible take the position that fallen angels and demons are one and the same. Yet, some Scripture shows a contrast. Both 2 Peter 2:4 and Jude 6 state fallen angels who kept not their first estate are reserved in everlasting chains under darkness unto the judgment of the great day. However, demons can be active here on earth or contained in the abyss. When Jesus cast the demons out of the man at Gerasa (Luke 8:26-34), they partitioned Jesus to not cast them into the abyss but allow them to enter into the swine. Demons are unclean, violent, and malicious (Matthew 8:28; 9:33; 10:1). They know Jesus as the most high God and recognize and respond to His supreme authority as shown in the Matthew account with the swine. They know their final, eternal state and inflict as much physical malady on mankind as they can (Matthew 12:22). They have all of the characteristics of Satan their leader. The major difference between Jesus, son of Mary in the Quran and Jesus, Son of God in the Bible is Jesus Christ has complete authority over Satan and his host of angels and demons. The Jesus of the Quran is only a messenger with limited authority.

CHAPTER VIII
WHO ARE THE UNBELIEVERS ACCORDING TO THE QURAN?

Unbelievers, according to the Quran, are anyone who does not worship Allah and accept and follow the Quran. Muslims are not to take an unbeliever as a friend—especially a Jew or a Christian. If a Muslim does make friends with either Jew, Christian, or a non-Muslim, they are counted as an unbeliever and subject to the wrath of Allah. The Quran takes the disassociation with the unbeliever much further than denouncing friendship; it commands the "true" Muslim to kill the unbeliever. The logic is the unbeliever is the worst of all creatures (beast). The following Surah verses provide the context of the unbeliever and how the Muslims are to treat unbelievers:

1. Surah 8:56 (page 203): "Surely the worst of beast in Allah's sight is the unbelievers."

2. Surah 98:5 (page 346): "The unbelievers of the people of the Book (Bible) and the idolaters shall be in the fire of Ghenna therein dwelling forever; those are the worst of creatures."

3. Surah 3:27 (page 76): "Let not the believers take the unbelievers for friends, rather than the believers for whoso does that belongs not to Allah in anything."

4. Surah 5:19 (page 130): "They are unbelievers who say Allah is the messiah Mary's son: say 'who then shall overrule Allah in any way if he desires to destroy the messiah Mary's son, and his mother, and all those who are on earth?'"

5. Surah 5:56 (page 136): "O believers take not Jews and Christians as friends, they are friends of each other, whoso of you makes them his friends is one of them, Allah guides not the people of evildoers."

6. Surah 5:76 (page 139): "They are unbelievers who say 'Allah is the messiah, Mary's son.'"

7. Surah 5:77 (page 140): "They are unbelievers who say 'Allah is the third of three.' No god is there but one Allah."

8. Surah 9:30 (page 210): "The Jews say, 'Ezra is the Son of Allah'; the Christians say, 'The messiah is the son of Allah.' That is the utterance of their mouths, conforming with the unbelievers before them. Allah assail them! How they are perverted!"

9. Surah 9:125 (page 222): "O believers, fight the unbelievers who are near to you and let

them find in you a harshness, and know that Allah is with the god fearing."

10. Surah 47:4 (page 220): "When you meet the unbelievers, smite their necks, then, when you have made wide slaughter among them tie fast the bonds."

11. Surah 9:5 (page 207):

Then, when the sacred months are drawn away, slay the idolaters wherever you find them, and take them, and confine them, and lie in wait for them at every place of ambush. But if they repent, and perform the prayer and pay the alms, then let them go their way; Allah is All-forgiving, All-compassionate.

12. Surah 9:29 (page 210): "Fight those who believe not in Allah and the last day and do not forbid what Allah and his messenger hath forbidden. Such men as practice not the religion of truth."

13. Surah 8:12 (page 198): "I (Allah) shall cast into the unbeliever's hearts terror, so smite above the necks and smite every finger of them."

14. Surah 3:60 (page 83): "No; Abraham in truth was not a Jew, neither a Christian; but he was a Muslim and one pure of faith; certainly he was never of the idolaters."

15. Surah 5:85 (page 141): "Thou wilt surely find the most hostile of men to the believers are the Jews and idolaters."

The major themes of these verses are: no affiliation with the non-Muslim by the Muslim, kill the non-Muslim when the opportunity arises and create as much terror as possible in the process. Some parts of these instructions are being carried out all over the world where Muslims are in contact with non-Muslims. Terrorist attacks against non-Muslims have occurred in almost every country where Muslims have a presence among non-Muslims. According to a list of Islamic terrorist attacks from 1983 through August 2016, over fifty countries have experienced Islamic terrorist attacks. There could be no greater doctrinal difference between the believer of the Quran and the believer of the Bible. Believers, according to the Bible, are those who accept Jesus as Lord and Savior. Believers, according to the Quran, must reject Jesus to have any hope of entering paradise. These verses firmly illustrate why there is little, if any, possibility of assimilation of Muslims into other societies. The verses also illustrate why Islam is in no way a religion of peace!

Muslims Killing Muslims

There is legitimacy to the statement that more Muslims are killed by fellow Muslims than all other non-Muslim groups combined. Is this religious paradox in some way encouraged by Quranic doctrine? A recent example occurred on Tuesday, February 3, 2015. According to both CNN and CBS news reports, an ISIS video surfaced showing the twenty-seven-year-old Pilot Lieutenant Moath al-Kasasbeh being burned alive in a steel cage by ISIS fighters.[14] According to the reports, al-Kasasbeh was a fighter pilot in the Royal Jordanian Air Force who was shot down while conducting air strikes against ISIS strongholds near Raqqa, Syria. He was part of the US-led coalition against ISIS. Jordan had played a pivotal part in the US-led coalition, but it was not a popular war within Jordan.[15]

According to the reports, Moath al-Kasasbeh was a devout Sunni Muslim who memorized the Quran, but that made no difference to the Sunni Muslims that made up the self-proclaimed ISIS caliphate. So, what is the justification? Referencing the Quranic verses Surah 3:27, Surah 5:56, and Surah 9:125, the act of taking or making a friend of an unbeliever by a Muslim relegates that Muslim to the status of an unbeliever (Jew, Christian, infidel). That person is then deserving of death and no longer belongs to Allah. The Jordanian pilot in the eyes of ISIS was treated as an unbeliever because he was part of a US-led coalition of infidels. To justify terrorist attacks and the barbaric acts that follow, ISIS, as well as other Islamic radicals, quickly draw from the Quran to play the unbeliever card.

The Emigration Tactic to Infiltrate and Destroy the Unbeliever

As Muhammad emigrated from Mecca to Medina and subdued two of the three Jewish groups and

---

[14] CBS/AP "Jordanian pilot's obscene burning death by ISIS sparks outrage in Mideast" 2015.

[15] Smith-Spark, and Martinez "Who was Jordanian pilot Moath al-Kasasbeh, killed by ISIS?".

destroyed the third, Muhammad's writings in the Quran encourages Muslims to do likewise. The tactic presented in the Quran is to infiltrate, overrun, subdue, and destroy the unbeliever by initial peaceful emigration into the unbeliever's territory. After emigration and when the Muslims grow sufficiently strong, the process begins. That is exactly what Muhammad did in Medina. Surah 4:97 (page 115) states: "Allah has preferred in rank those who struggle with their possessions and their selves over the ones who sit at home; yet to each Allah has promised the reward most fair; and Allah has preferred those who struggle over the ones who sit at home for the bounty of a mighty wage." This is followed by Surah 4:100: "Whoso emigrates in the way of Allah will find in the earth many refuges and plenty; whoso goes forth from his house and emigrant to Allah and His Messenger, and then death overtakes him, his wage shall have fallen on Allah; surely Allah is All-forgiving, All-compassionate." These verses clearly encourage the Muslim to emigrate into foreign societies and as a result they are promised a mighty wage. The Muslim emigrant is preferred by Allah over the Muslim who does not. The answer to the question of why Muslims pouring through Libya in 2016 are emigrating to Europe and the US rather than to other Muslim countries is found in these Quranic verses. It is amazing that in the year 2016 leaders in Europe and the US appear to be ignorant of a tactic that has been deployed since the time of Muhammad. The Muslim communities throughout Europe and the world that have emigrated from a Muslim homeland to non-Muslim countries have two things in common. First, they appear to be eager to emigrate, but seem to never assimilate into any other society. Second, even with second and third generation adults, there appears to always be controversy and terrorism that follow. The participants in the Boston marathon bombing, the San Bernardino massacre, and the Fort Hood shooting fall into this lack of generation assimilation. The aggression is always against the non-Muslim.

Encouragement to Deceive the Unbeliever

According to the Quran, the Muslim is allowed to lie, deceive, and cheat the unbeliever with impunity. There are forms of lying to non-Muslims that is permitted in Islam. The most prevalent of this form of lying is called *taqiyya*. This is lying to advance the cause of Islam. History of Muhammad's excursions and battles reveal the use of this lying and deception to gain the trust of non-Muslims in order to discover weaknesses and vulnerabilities so that they could be defeated. Several verses in the Quran provide context:

1. Surah 3:28 (page 76) councils the Muslim to lie to the non-Muslim if they fear them.
2. Surah 3:46 (Note 3:54 in other translations) (page 81): "And they (the unbelievers) schemed and Allah schemed (against them) and Allah is the best of schemers."

The Arabic word used for scheme or plot is *makara*. Remember, *makara* correctly translated from an Arabic dictionary means to deceive, delude, cheat, double-cross, double-dealing. Simply put, if

Allah is the supreme deceiver, then lying and deceit for the Muslim to the non-Muslim *taqiyya* is perfectly acceptable. The example *makara* by Allah is mirrored by the Muslim follower *taqiyya*.

In some Hadith, the use of lies and deceit by Muhammad is revealed. Bukchari 52:269: The prophet (Muhammad) said, "War is deceit." The context of this statement is thought to be the murder of Usayr ibn Zarim and his thirty unarmed men by Muhammad's men after he guaranteed them safe passage. Muhammad again demonstrated *taqiyya* or *makara* when he signed a ten-year treaty with the Meccans that allowed him access to their city while he secretly prepared his forces for a takeover. He broke the treaty and conquered Mecca two years later.

Taqiyya Today

Today, leaders of the Muslim world say one thing to English-speaking audiences and say something entirely different to their own people. Yasser Arafat of the Palestinian Authority was well known for this type of deception. More recently, the Iran Nuclear Deal and the $400 million ransom payment to Iran for hostages falls into this category. The West continues to get duped by Islamic states. This has not been the case with Israel. They understand that any agreement, especially at state level, between Muslim and non-Muslim is not considered binding by the Muslim state *makara* was well demonstrated by Muhammad and has been continued throughout the ages and continues today. The Islamic Society of North America insists it has not ever been involved with the Muslim

Brotherhood. In fact, it was created by the Muslim Brotherhood and has bankrolled Hamas. The Council on American Islamic Relations (CAIR) is well known for its ties to terror.

Finally, American cleric Anwar al-Awlaki was regularly sought out by National Public Radio (NPR), PBS, and even government leaders to expound on the peaceful nature of Islam. Of course, he was part of the plot in the Fort Hood massacre and the attempt to blow up a Detroit bound airliner. Al-Awlaki was killed by a US drone strike in Yemen. His deception caught up with him. Truly, Muslims who deal deceitfully and commit such atrocities as mass-murder and beheadings of the unbeliever is simply following the Quran. This is not radical Islam; it is just Islam.

How Should a Christian Treat a Muslim?

Jesus said in Matthew 5:44 "Love your enemies, bless them that curse you, do good to them that hate you, pray for them who despitefully use you and persecute you". In verses 39-41 of Matthew 5, Jesus is speaking to the disciples as to how they are to respond to those who attack them personally. When one smites you turn the other cheek. When one sues you give that person your coat and cloak, When one compels you to go a mile go two. The response is one-on-one, person-to-person that you may be blameless and a good witness to your enemy.

However, a Christian response to the teaching of false doctrine and perversion of the truth is totally different. In Matthew 23:5-37, Jesus taught the disciples concerning the false doctrine of the Pharisees.

Jesus pronounced seven woes on the Pharisees calling them a generation of vipers and said how could they escape the damnation of hell? In Acts 13:16-17 Paul confronted Elymas (Bar-Jesus) for attempting to lead Paulus away from the faith. Paul called Elymas the **enemy** of righteousness and through the power of the Holy Spirit blinded Elymas. In Jude 3-19, Jude exhorts the Christians to earnestly contend for the faith and warns them of those who would deny the Lord Jesus is God. In Acts 8:9-24 Peter told Simon who used sorcery to bewitch the people of Samaria to repent for attempting to purchase the power of the Holy Spirit in laying on of hands. The God of the bible does not tolerate the distortion and corruption of his word!

Therefore, the duty of a Christian is to love their enemies with a godly love (tough love, agape love) while confronting those who spread false doctrine and pervert the truth. God's love does not mean tolerance and never allows for the compromise of his word.

CHAPTER IX
WHAT CONSTITUTES
A MARTYR?

According to the Quran and the Hadith

Martyrdom, according to the Quran, is a noble act. In the United States, many questions arising from the Fort Hood shooting, the Boston Marathon bombing, the San Bernardino massacre, and the Orlando gay night club massacre and other less publicized atrocities have been posed, analyzed, and discussed. In most cases, the basic reason is either ignored or the result of ignorance of those submitting opinions.

Why would a military officer rush into a group of military personnel shouting, *"Allahu akbar"* while firing a .45-caliber pistol with the intent to kill as many fellow service men and woman as possible? It took the Obama administration six-years to acknowledge the Fort Hood shooting was a terrorist attack.[16]

---

[16] Goodenough "Six years Later",2015.

Why would it take six years to admit the act was not workplace violence when it was so obvious to all?

Why would a husband and wife with a child risk all, including death, to kill fellow workers in support of ISIS? *The Los Angeles Times* provides the key points in an article titled, "San Bernardino Shooting Updates, December 9, 2015."[17]

Why would a teenager and his older brother create bombs using pressure cookers to kill and maim innocent bystanders regardless of age or gender? The facts are presented in a news article by CNN titled, "Boston Marathon Terror Attack Fast Facts."[18]

Why would a man with possible indications of being homosexual who frequented a gay night club decide to enter it on a crowded night and kill and wound dozens of people? The motive is presented in multiple articles with one of particular interest published June 14, 2016 by **PalmBeachPost.com** titled "Orlando shooter Omar Mateen was gay, former classmate says."[19]

Internationally, why would Europe's first woman suicide bomber, twenty-six-year-old Hasna Aitboulahcen (a somewhat morally loose woman), in an attempt to lure French Police into position to kill, detonate a suicide vest, killing herself? According to an article in *The Guardian* by Kim Willsher on November 20, 2015, neighbors of Hasna said, "She

[17] Welsh and Barboza "San Bernardino shooting updates", 2015.
[18] CNN Library "Boston Marathon Terror Attack Fast Facts", 2016.
[19] Mower "Orlando shooter Omar Mateen was gay, former classmate says", 2016.

didn't look like a suicide bomber and she drank alcohol." Another neighbor in Paris said "she was a 'tomboy' who dressed in jeans, trainers, and a black hat until she began wearing a hijab a month" before her suicide.[20]

Considering all of these atrocious acts, what is the common thread? Are they crazy, radical extremist, Muslim extremist, or just following what the Quran teaches?

The unbelievers according to the Quran are Jews, Christians, and anyone who does not worship Allah, believe His messenger Muhammad, and abide by the Quran. The target priorities are Jews first, Christians second, followed by infidels. To understand the magnitude of Islamic terrorist attacks domestically and internationally, research was conducted using the US State Department Country Reports on Terrorism, Historic Timeline from National Counter-terrorism Center. The Counter Terrorism Center's report on Islamist terrorist attacks provides tremendous insight into the magnitude of these deadly attacks and the activity of these extremist.[21] From year 2000 through year 2015, over 12,500 people were killed and over 14,000 were injured as a result of these attacks. Many of the Muslim attackers were martyred accompanied by celebration of their sponsor. During the time period, forty-two countries experienced 318 attacks with Israel near the top of the list. Israel was and

---

[20] Willsher "Hasna Aitboulahcen: police examine remains of 'cowgirl' turned suicide bonber", 2015.

[21] National Counter Terrorism Center "Historical Time Line 2000-2015".

continues to be a prime target. The following Surah verses provide the context for the encouragement of terrorist attacks:

1. Surah 5:56 (page 136): "O believers take not Jews and Christians as friends, they are friends of each other, whoso of you makes them his friends is one of them, Allah guides not the people of evildoers."

2. Surah 9:29 (page 210): "Fight those who believe not in Allah and the last day and do not forbid what Allah and his messenger hath forbidden. Such men as practice not the religion of truth."

3. Surah 47:4 (page 220): "When you meet the unbelievers, smite their necks, then, when you have made wide slaughter among them tie fast the bonds."

4. Surah 9:125 (page 222): "O believers, fight the unbelievers who are near to you and let them find in you a harshness, and know that Allah is with the god fearing."

5. Surah 9:112 (page 220) makes this clear. "Allah has bought from the believers their selves and their possessions against the gift of paradise; they fight in the way of Allah; they kill and are killed; **that is a promise binding upon Allah** in the Torah, and the Gospel and the Koran and who fulfils his covenant truer than Allah?"

The clear message from the Quran is the unbeliever is any non-Muslim. The Muslim is to fight and kill the unbeliever. If the Muslim is killed (martyred) during the process, Allah is obligated to receive them into Paradise. Other verses from the Quran that establish martyrdom include:

1. Surah 4:71 (page 110): "Whosoever obeys Allah and the Messenger – they are with those whom Allah has blessed, prophets, just men, **martyrs**, the righteous; good companions they!"

2. Surah 3:152 (page 93): "If you are slain or die in Allah's way forgiveness and mercy from Allah are a better thing than that you amass. Surely if you die or are slain, it is unto Allah you shall be mustered."

3. Surah 3:194: "And those who emigrated and were expelled from their habitations, those who suffered hurt in my way, and fought, and were slain – them I shall surly acquit of their evil deeds and I shall admit them to gardens underneath which rivers flow."

4. Surah 4:75 (page 111): "So let them fight in the way of Allah who sell the present life for the world to come; and whosoever fights in the way of Allah and is slain or conquers. We shall bring him a mighty wage."

5. Surah 47:5-10: "And those who are slain in the way of Allah, He will not send their works astray. He will guide them, and dispose their minds aright, and he will admit them to paradise that He has made known to them."

So, why would a Muslim, possible homosexual male, who according to Islam, would be bound for hell, kill the "unbeliever" and why would a loose Muslim woman blow herself up in an attempt to kill unbelievers? The answer is Allah has a binding promise to give them the gift of Paradise. The Quran makes it clear if you are a marginal Muslim, your "get out of hell free card" and your ticket to Paradise is through killing the unbeliever.

Many people are attracted to these ideals because it is works-based. Works for salvation is prominent in many religions and even Christians can be lured into this trap. I was recently asked by a friend of mine (who I believe is a Christian but from a denomination not given too much Bible Study) the question, "I have heard if a person who is not a Christian dies, like a policeman or fireman, while doing a good deed, they will go to heaven; what do you think?" My answer was of course *no*! I followed up with John 14:6: "Jesus saith unto him, 'I am the way, the truth, and the life; no man cometh unto the Father but by me.'" If a novice Christian asks this type of question, we must realize how easy it is for people to embrace a works-based salvation when they are lacking the truth.

Further Fringe Benefits from Martyrdom

From the Al-miqdam ibn Ma'dikarib Hadith, we see the additional benefits of being a martyr:

Allah's messenger (Muhammad) (peace be upon him) said, "The martyr receives six good things from Allah: he is forgiven the first shedding of blood; he is shown his abode in paradise; he is preserved from the punishment in the grave; he is kept safe from the greatest terror; he has placed on his head the crown of honor, a ruby of which is better than the world and what it contains; he is married to seventy-two wives of the maidens with large dark eyes, and is made intercessor for seventy of his relatives."

Why Do Family Members Celebrate Martyrdom of a Son?

When a Muslim is martyred while committing murder in the name of Allah or defending the name of Muhammad, you see celebration by the family members more than remorse or any type of apology. Why is that? The answer is found in the above reference (Ma'dikarib Hadith). If one is killed while killing infidels, Christians, or Jews, then he gets seventy "get out of hell free passes" for his family. This puts jubilance in the hearts of fathers, mothers, brothers, sisters, wives, and children of the martyr.

Works Unto Death!

The common theme through all of the aforementioned atrocities is what is taught in Islam: a works-based religion. Truly works unto death. Therefore, rather than listen to endless analysis from people who either have no clue or are purposely misleading go to the source of the motivation. The source is the Quran and the Hadith. Martyrs in the Bible such as Stephen, Paul, and James, the brother of John, were slain for trying to lead men to Jesus Christ. Martyrs in the Quran inherit Paradise, seventy-two virgins and receive seventy "get out of hell free passes" for being killed while killing those who preach the gospel. What a contrast in doctrine and belief!

CHAPTER X
WHO ARE MESSENGERS FROM ALLAH AND WHAT ARE THE SIGNS AUTHENTICATING THEM?

According to the Quran, Allah appointed both angels and man to be his messengers. The following Surah verses provides a list along with an indication of the messenger's responsibilities and status:

1. Surah 35:2 (page 138): "Praise belongs to Allah, originator of the heavens and earth, who appointed the angels to be messengers having wings two, three and four, increasing creation as he wills."

2. Surah 2:81 (page 39): "And We gave Moses the Book and after him sent succeeding messengers, and we gave Jesus Son of Mary the clear signs."

3. Surah 4:16 (page 102): "Whoso obeys Allah and His Messenger He will admit him to gardens underneath which rivers flow."
4. Surah 4:83 (page 112): "Whoso obeys the messenger, thereby obeys Allah."
5. Surah 4:135 (page 120): "O believers, believe in Allah, and His messengers and the Book He has sent down on His messengers and the book which He sent down before."
6. Surah 4:162 (page 124):

We have revealed to thee as We revealed to Noah, and the prophets after him, and We revealed to Abraham, Ishmael, Isaac, Jacob, and the tribes, Jesus and Job, Jonah and Aaron and Solomon, and we gave David psalms and Messengers We have already told thee of before, and Messengers We have not told thee of; and unto Moses Allah spoke directly- Messengers bearing good tidings, and warning, So that mankind might have no argument against Allah, after the Messengers; Allah is All-mighty and All-wise.

7. Surah 6:83-85 (page 159):

That is Our argument, which We bestowed upon Abraham as against his people. We raise up in degrees whom We will; surely thy Lord is All-wise, All-knowing. And We gave to him Isaac and Jacob- each one We guided. And Noah We guided before; and of his seed

David and Solomon, Job and Joseph. Moses and Aaron- even so We recompense the good-doers- Zachariah and John, Jesus and Elias; each was of the righteous; Ishmael and Elisha, Jonah and Lot- each one We preferred above all beings; and of their fathers, and of their seed, and of their brethren; and We elected them, and We guided them to a straight path.

8. Surah 8:28 (page 200): "O believers, betray not Allah and the Messenger, and betray not your trusts and that wittingly; and know that your wealth and your children are a trial, and that with Allah is a mighty wage."

9. Surah 9:63 (page 214): "Those who hurt Allah's Messenger – for them awaits a painful chastisement."

10. Surah 8:42 (page 201): "Know that, whatever booty you take, the fifth of it is Allah's and the messenger's."

11. Surah 8:2 (page 197): "They will question thee concerning the spoils. Say: 'The spoils belong to Allah and the Messenger; so fear you Allah. And set things right between you, and obey you Allah and His Messenger if you are believers.'"

12. Surah 3:137 (page 91): "Muhammad is naught but a messenger, messengers have passed away before him."

13. Surah 33:40 (page 126): "Muhammad is not the father of any one of you men, but the messenger of Allah and the Seal of the Prophets."

From these verses, several messages are emphasized to the believers. Muhammad is counted with all previous messengers, prophets, and patriarchs of the Bible and some of Arabic legend. As previously stated in Surah 33:40 (page 126): Muhammad is the final authority (Seal of the Prophets) over all given by Allah. "Muhammad is not the father of any one of you men, but the messenger of Allah and the Seal of the Prophets." Good Muslims are to obey Muhammad as they would obey Allah. With Islam being spread primarily with the sword, after destroying the unbeliever and taking the spoils, from twenty percent to the entire take belongs to the Messenger (Muhammad) and Allah.

The Quran conveys many of the Bible encounters of the prophets and patriarchs of the Old and New Testament. Many times, the God of the Bible authenticated the message of these people with significant signs (miracles). Sometimes, inaccurate versions of these signs are presented in the Quran. However, the very foundation that Muhammad uses to convey his authority as the "Seal of the Prophets" is not authenticated by any significant sign. The consequences of not heeding the "signs" are stated in numerous Surahs. They can be summed up with two verses: Surah 10:6-7 (page 225: "Surely those who look not to encounter Us and are well-pleased with the present life and are at rest in it, and those who are heedless of Our Signs, those- their refuge is the Fire, for that they have been earning."

Surah 7:38 (page 175):

Those that cry lies to Our signs and wax proud
against them- the gates of heaven shall not be
opened to them; nor shall they enter Paradise
until the camel passes through the eye of the
needle. Even so We recompense the sinners;
Gehenna shall be their cradle above them cov-
erings. Even so We recompense the evildoers.

**Signs That are Recast From the Bible to the
Quran Include the Following:**
1.   Surah 7:101 (page 184): "Then We sent, after
     them Moses with Our signs to Pharaoh and his
     council but they did them wrong."
2.   Followed by Surah 7:103-114:

Moses said, "Pharaoh, I am a Messenger form the
Lord of all Being, worthy to say nothing regarding
Allah except the truth. I have brought a clear sign
to you from your Lord; so send forth with me the
Children of Israel.' Said he, 'If thou hast brought a
SIGN, produce it, if thou speakest truly.' So he cast
his staff; and behold it was a serpent manifest."

**The problem with the serpent sign is according to
Exodus 7:1-13 it was Aaron who cast the rod that
became a serpent—not Moses!**
3.   Surah 7:130 (page 186): "So We lose upon
     them the flood and the locusts, the lice and
     the frogs, the blood. Distinct signs; but they
     waxed proud and were a sinful people."

The problem with the flood sign is that it did not happen. A flood was not one of the ten plagues God brought upon Pharaoh and the Egyptians (Exodus 7:14-12:30).

4. Surah 17:103 (page 314): "And we gave Moses nine signs. Clear signs. Ask the Children of Israel when he came to them and Pharaoh said to him, 'Moses, I think thou art accursed.'"

The problem with the nine signs is there were ten, signs not nine (blood, frogs, gnats, flies, livestock, boils, hail and fire, locusts, darkness, death of the first born).

5. Surah 23:52 (page 40): "We made Mary's son and his mother, to be a sign, and gave them refuge upon a height, where a hollow was and a spring."

The problem with this Surah is the Bible never speaks of Mary being a Sign to anyone and Jesus was surely not a sign; according to the Bible, He is the Son of God, not the son of Allah. Further, Jesus did many miracles to authenticate who he was. Jesus said in John 10:30, "I and my Father are one." Jesus also said in John 14:6, "I am the way, the truth, and the life; no man cometh unto the Father but by Me."

6. Surah 42:28, 31 (page 196):

And of His signs is the creation of the heavens and earth and the crawling things He has scattered abroad in them; and He is able to gather them whenever He will. ... And of his signs are the ships that run on the sea like landmarks; and if He wills, He stills the wind, and they remain motionless on its back.

The creation in no way validates Muhammad's message and the fact that ships sail on water conveys no prophetic message.

7. Surah 2:183 (page 52): "Wherein the Koran was sent down to be a guidance to the people, and as clear signs of the Guidance to the Salvation..."

Nothing is clear about the Koran. The only authenticating signs come from the Bible and when they are recast in the Koran, most have some type of error.

Other signs mentioned in many of the Surahs include the creation: night, day, the heavens, sun, moon, stars, rain, and crops. From these signs, even a novice would have difficulty believing a man recasting with error the signs presented in the Bible, while providing for himself no sign as a prophet?

Biblical Signs Authenticating Jesus as God the Son

There are no signs or miracles given in the Quran to authenticate the authority and position of Muhammad. Some statements of miracles that Jesus, son of Mary would do are mentioned in the Quran. None are specific. However, there are many recorded in the gospels that authenticate the power, authority, and position of Jesus, the Son of God. In the gospels, Jesus demonstrates His power and position **over**

demons by casting them out at Capernaum (Luke 4:31-37), at Gadara in Luke 8:26-40, and healing a demon possessed boy in Luke 11:14. Jesus demonstrated His power **over nature** when He stilled the wind and the water in Luke 8:22-25. Jesus demonstrated numerus times His power **over sickness and disease** in Luke 5:12-26; 6:6-12; 7:1-10; 8:41-56; 18:35-43. Jesus demonstrated His power **over death** by raising a widow's son from the dead in Luke 7:11-18 and raising Lazarus from the dead in John 11:40-44. Even greater is Jesus who conquered death by His own resurrection recorded in Matthew 28:6. Jesus foretold His resurrection in John 2:19 when He told the Jews who sought a sign to "Destroy this temple (His body) and in three days I will raise it up." That is exactly what Jesus did. There is no greater authentication sign than that of victory over the grave!

CHAPTER XI
DISCREPANCIES OF EVENTS IN THE QURAN COMPARED TO BIBLICAL HISTORY

E rrors and inconsistencies were prevalent when comparing the signs in the Quran to the actual accounts in the Bible. The same is true when comparing the lives and actions of many of the well-known individuals listed in the Old and New Testaments. A small sample selected for comparison include Noah, Abraham, Isaac, Ishmael, Moses, Saul, Solomon, Zachariah, the apostles of Jesus and the Samaritans.

Noah

In Surah 11, the writings by Muhammad indicate one of Noah's sons drowned in the flood. Surah 11:41-42:

So it ran with them amid waves like mountains; and Noah called to his son, who was standing apart, "Embark with us, my son, and be thou not with the unbelievers!" He said, "I will take refuge in a mountain that shall defend me from the water." Said he, "Today there is no defender from Allah's command but for him on whom He has mercy." And the waves came between them, and he was among the drowned.

Genesis 6:18: "And Noah begot three sons, Shem, Ham, and Japheth."

Genesis 10:22-23 records Noah's sin after the flood where all three sons are involved in the event:

And Ham, the father of Canaan saw the nakedness of his father, and told his two brethren outside. And Shem and Japheth took a garment, and laid it upon both their shoulders, and went backward, and covered the nakedness of their father; and their faces were backward, and they saw not their father's nakedness.

Three sons were born before the flood and the same three sons lived after the flood. **No son of Noah drowned!**

Abraham:

1. Surah 3:57-60 (page 82-83):

People of the Book (Bible)! Why do you dispute concerning Abraham? The Torah was not sent down, neither the Gospel, but after him. What have you no reason? Ha, you are the ones who dispute on what you know; why then dispute you touching a matter of which you know not anything: Allah knows, and you know not. NO; Abraham in truth was not a Jew, neither a Christian; but he was a Muslim and one pure of faith; certainly he was never of the idolaters.

Of course, Judaism and Christianity precede Islam by hundreds of years. Reference to the Jews is first recorded in 2 Kings 16:6 in the days of King Ahaz of the Southern Kingdom and King Pekah of the Northern Kingdom. Followers of Jesus Christ were first called Christians at Antioch (Acts 11:26) approximately AD 60. Muhammad, the Quran, and Islam surfaced AD 610.

2.   Surah 21:52-70 (page 21-22) records an episode of Abraham confronting his father and his people for serving Idols. Abraham is said to have broken their Idols into fragments (Surah 21:59). When they confronted Abraham, they decided to burn him but Allah (We) intervened and made the fire cool. Surah 21:68-70 states: "They said, 'Burn him, and help your gods, if you would do aught.' We said; O fire, be coolness and safety for Abraham!' They desired to outwit him; so We made them the more losers, and We delivered him, and Lot unto the land that We had blessed for all beings."

No such record of Abraham is recorded in the Bible. The above episode parallels two records in the

Bible: That of Gideon destroying his father's and his people's idols of Baal in Judges 6:25-32 and Daniel's three companions in Daniel 3:1-28 who were cast into the furnace Nebuchadnezzar had prepared for those refusing to worship the image he had setup. Wonder if there was a mix up?

3. The Kaaba is the most sacred shrine of the Muslims, a small structure, containing a black stone, in the courtyard of the great Mosque at Mecca. It is the point toward which Muslims face when praying and the goal of the *hajj* or pilgrimage. The Quran states Abraham and Ishmael built the Kaaba.

Surah 2:117-118 (page 43):

And when his Lord tested Abraham with certain words, and he fulfilled them. He said, "Behold, I make you a leader for the people." Said he, "and of my seed?" He said "My covenant shall not reach the evildoers." And when We appointed the House (Kaaba) to be a place of visitation of the people and a sanctuary, and: "Take to yourselves Abraham's station for a place of prayer." **And We made covenant with Abraham and Ishmael**.

Surah 2:122 (page 44): "And when Abraham, and Ishmael with him raised up the foundations of the House: 'Our Lord, receive this from us.'"

Finally, in Surah 5:97 (page 143): "Allah has appointed the Kaaba, the Holy House, as an establishment for men, and the holy month, the offering, and the necklaces – that, that you may know that Allah knows all that is in the heavens and in the earth, and Allah has knowledge of everything."

First of all, according to the Bible, no covenant was ever established between Ishmael and the God of the Bible. This is what is said of Ishmael in Genesis 16:11-12:

> And the angel of the Lord said unto her (Hagar), "Behold, thou art with child, and shalt bear a son, and shalt call his mane Ishmael; because the Lord hath heard thy affliction. And he will be a wild man; his hand will be against every man. And every man's hand against him; and he shall dwell in the presence of all his brethren."

Second, Ishmael was rejected by the God of the Bible to be the covenant bearer and covenant nation. Genesis 17:18-19: "And Abraham said unto God, 'Oh that Ishmael might live before thee!' And God said, 'Sarah, thy wife, shall bear thee a son indeed; and I will establish my covenant with him for an everlasting covenant and with his seed after him.'"

Third, when Isaac was born Hagar and her son Ishmael were cast out from Abraham, Sarah, and Isaac. Genesis 21:9-14:

> And Sarah saw the son of Hagar, the Egyptian, whom she had borne unto Abraham, mocking.

Wherefore she said unto Abraham, "Cast out this bondwoman and her son, for the son of this bondwoman shall not be heir with my son, even with Isaac." And God said unto Abraham, "Let it not be grievous in thy sight because of the lad, and because of thy bond-woman; in all that Sarah hath said unto thee, hearken unto her voice; for in Isaac shall thy seed be called."

Genesis 21:14 records Abraham sending Ishmael and Hagar out. God does not change His mind. He is the same yesterday, today, and forever (Hebrews 13:8).

Fourth, with the instructions from God and Sarah's position on Ishmael, it is not likely that Abraham would participate in building any place of worship that went contrary to God's plan and Sarah's wishes.

Isaac

Surah 37:100-103 page 153-154: "And when he (Isaac) had reached the age of running with him (Abraham), he said 'My son, I see in a dream that I shall sacrifice thee; consider what thinkest thou.' He said, 'my father does as thou art bidden; thou shalt find me, Allah willing, one of the steadfast.'"

This is inconsistent with what the Bible says. Genesis 22:7-8: "And Isaac spoke unto Abraham his father, and said, 'My father: and he said, here am I, my son.' And he said, 'Behold the fire and the wood: but where is the lamb for a burnt offering?' And Abraham said, 'My son, God will provide himself a lamb for a burnt offering:' so, they went both together."

The Bible records no dream. God spoke directly to Abraham (Genesis 22:1). No dialogue between Abraham and Isaac regarding Isaac becoming the sacrifice took place.

Moses

Surah 28:2 (page 86): "We will recite to thee something of the tidings of Moses and Pharaoh truthfully, for a people who believe."

Surah 28:6: "So We revealed to Moses' mother, 'Suckle him, then, when thou fearest for him, cast him into the sea, and do not fear, neither sorrow, for We shall return him to thee, and shall appoint him one of the Envoys.'"

Surah 28:8: "Said Pharaoh's wife, 'He will be a comfort to me and thee. Slay him not; perchance he will profit us, or we will take him for a son.'"

First, the infant Moses was not cast into the sea. He was placed in a waterproof basket by his mother and placed in the river's edge near where Pharaoh's daughter came down to bathe (Exodus 2:3).

Second, it was not Pharaoh's wife who found and took Moses and raised him as her son; it was Pharaoh's daughter (Exodus 2:5-10).

Joseph:

1. In Surah 12:30-32, Muhammad writes certain women talked about Potiphar's wife after she had tried to seduce Joseph. Muhammad writes:

Certain women that were in the city said, "The Governor's wife has been soliciting her page; he smote her heart with love; we see her in manifest error." When she heard their sly whispers, she sent to them, and made ready for them a repast, then she gave to each one of them a knife. "Come forth, attend to them," she said. And when they saw him, they so admired him that they cut their hands, saying, "Allah save us! This is no mortal; he is no other but a noble angel."

There is no record in the Bible of this ever happening.

2. In Surah 12:42, Muhammad writes concerning the dreams that Joseph interpreted for Pharaoh's butler and baker. "Fellow-prisoners, as for one of you, he shall pour wine for his lord; as for the other, he shall **be crucified**, and birds will eat of his head. The matter is decided whereon you enquire."

The Bible says in Genesis 40:22: "But he hanged the chief baker: as Joseph, had interpreted to them." Hanged, not crucified!

3. In Surah 12:4, Muhammad writes: "When Joseph said to his father, 'Father, I saw eleven stars, and the sun and the moon; I saw them bowing down before me.'"

In Surah 12:100, Muhammad writes:

So, when they entered unto Joseph, he took his father and mother in to his arms saying, "enter you into Egypt, if Allah will in security." And he lifted his father and mother upon the throne; and the others fell down prostrate before him. "See, father," he said, "this is the interpretation of my vision of long ago, my Lord has made it true."

The Bible records in Genesis 35:18: "And it came to pass, as her soul was in departing (for she died), that she called his name Benoni; but his father called him Benjamin."

Rachel, the mother of Joseph and Benjamin, died at the birth of Benjamin years before Jacob, the father of Joseph, came down to Egypt. Rachel could not have gone to Egypt, for she was dead.

Saul

In Surah 2:249 (page 63), Muhammad records the sign of the kingship of Saul: "And their Prophet said to them, (the Israelites) 'the sign of his kingship is that the Ark will come to you, in it a Shechina from your Lord, (Allah), and a remnant of what the folk of Moses and Aaron's folk left behind, the angels bearing it.'"

The problem with this statement is the God of the Bible instructed only the seed of Levi, the Kohathites, to be in charge of the Ark (Numbers 3:31). The instructions included how the Ark was to be moved. This was violated when the Israelites moved the Ark on a wagon after the Philistines had captured it and returned. When Uzzah attempted to stabilize the Ark because the oxen shook the Ark, God killed him (2 Samuel 6:6-7). Never are angels instructed to bear the Ark. This was a symbol of God's presence among men, not angels.

Solomon:

1. In Surah 27:16, Solomon is said to be able to speak the language of birds. "And Solomon was David's heir, and he said, 'Men, we have been taught the speech of the birds, and we have been given of everything; surely this is indeed the manifest bounty.' And his hosts were mustered to Solomon, Jinn, men and birds, duly disposed."

2. In Surah 27:20-23, Solomon is said to have met the Queen of Sheba through the hoopoe bird:

And he (Solomon) reviewed the birds; then he said, "How is it with me, that I do not see the hoopoe: Or is he among the absent? Assuredly I will chastise him with a terrible chastisement, or I will slaughter him, or he bring me a clear authority." But he tarried not long, and said, "I have comprehended that which thou hast not comprehended, and I have come from Sheba to thee with a sure tiding. I found a woman ruling over them, and she has been given of everything, and she possesses a mighty throne. I found her and her people prostrating to the sun, apart from Allah."

Nowhere in the Bible is any statement that Solomon could speak and understand Bird Language.

In 1 Kings 10:1 is the record of the Queen of
Sheba coming to visit Solomon: "And when the queen
of Sheba heard of the fame of Solomon concerning
the Name of the Lord, she came to test him with hard
questions." No hoopoe bird is mentioned.

3. In Surah 34:10-15 (page 132), it is said the
   Jinn served Solomon as punishment and while
   they were working for him he died leaning
   on his staff. The jinn did not know he had
   died because Solomon continued leaning on
   his staff while dead. This ended when a beast
   (worm) came out of the ground and chewed
   Solomon's staff and it broke and Solomon fell
   to the ground. The Surah verses state:

And We made the Fount of Molten Brass to
flow for him. And of the jinn, some worked
before him by the leave of his Lord; and such
of them as swerved away from Our commandment, We would let them taste the chastisement of the Blaze; fashioning for him
whatsoever he would- places of worship,
statues, porringers, like water-troughs, and
anchored cooking-pots. "Labor, O House of
David, in thankfulness; for few indeed are
those that are thankful among My servants."
And when We decreed that he (Solomon)
should die. Naught indicated to them that he
was dead but the Beast of the Earth devouring
his staff; and when he fell down, the Jinn saw
clearly that, had they only known the Unseen,

they would not have continued in the humbling chastisement.

The Bible gives no record of any spiritual being serving Solomon and surely no record of him dying and remaining upright on his staff until a worm comes out of the ground and devoirs his staff and Solomon then falls to the ground.

Zachariah

In Surah 19:11, Muhammad writes of the visit of the angel announcing the birth of John the Baptist to him and Elisabeth. "He said, 'Lord appoint me some sign.' Said He, 'Thy sign is that thou shalt not speak to men through being without fault, three nights.'"

The Bible says in Luke 1:20 when Gabriel the angel addressed Zachariah, "And, behold, thou shalt be dumb, and not able to speak, until the day that these things shall be performed, because thou believest not my words, which shall be fulfilled in their season." The season was fulfilled when John was born and at that time Zachariah was able to speak. Luke 1:63-64 records this. "And he (Zachariah) asked for a writing tablet, and wrote saying, 'His name is John.' And they all marveled. And his mouth was opened immediately, and his tongue was loosed, and he spoke and praised God."

At least nine months passed; not three days!

Samaritan

In Surah 20:86-87 Muhammad writes:

Said He, "We (Allah) have tempted thy people since thou didst leave them. The Samaritan has misled them to error." Then Moses returned very angry and sorrowful to his people, saying, "My people did your lord not promise a fair promise to you? ... but we were loaded with fardels, even the ornaments of the people and we cast them, as the Samaritan also, threw them into the fire. Then he brought out for them a Calf, a mere body that lowed; and they said, 'This is your god, and the god of Moses whom he has forgotten.'"

This incident recorded in the Quran deals with Moses and the Children of Israel at Sinai when Moses received the Law. While Moses is up on Mount Sinai receiving the law, Allah (We) is tempting the people to sin. There are two things wrong with this picture: First, the God of the Bible tempts no one. James 1:13 says, **"Let no man say when he is tempted, I am tempted of God; for God cannot be tempted with evil, neither tempteth he any man**." Second, the Samaritan did not come on the scene until the Northern Kingdom was captured by Assyria and repopulated by King Shalmaneser of Assyria from 720 BC to 725 BC (2 Kings 17, 18). These transfers intermarried with some of the remaining Jews. They were called Samaritans. The account in Exodus 32 occurred between 1450 and 1410 BC. This is a 700-year discrepancy.

The Apostles of Jesus, Son of Mary

Surah 3:45: "And when Jesus perceived their unbelief, he said, 'Who will be my helpers unto Allah?' The Apostles said, 'We will be helpers of Allah; we believe in Allah witness thou our submission. Lord, we believe in that Thou hast sent down, and we follow the Messenger.'"

The Bible in Matthew 16:13-16 records Jesus asking His disciples (verse 13): "Who do men say that I, the Son of man, am?" Peter, one of the Apostles, replies in verse 16: "And Simon Peter answered and said, 'Thou art the Christ, the Son of the living God.'" This is an Apostle, Matthew, recording what Peter, an Apostle, said of Jesus. After the resurrection of Jesus, the Apostle John records the meeting between The Risen Christ and Thomas, another Apostle who had doubted Jesus was raised from the dead. When Jesus invited Thomas to thrust his hand into his side where the spear of the Roman soldiers had pierced and believe. Thomas replied in John 20:28, "And Thomas answered and said unto him, 'My Lord and my God.'"

These Apostles did not view Jesus as merely a messenger. They knew He was God the Son. They knew Jesus had been crucified, died, and raised from the dead.

Things to Think About

One is pressed to wonder why so many discrepancies. If a testament is inaccurate in the small things, how can it be trusted with weightier matters such as:

Who is the true and living God, who are the true prophets of God, salvation, and eternal life?

Mass distribution of the Old and New Testament did not take place until the invention of the printing press in 1455. Prior to the printing press, pain staking efforts and much time was spent by scribes to hand produce just one copy. Even if one was able to get a copy of some of the books like the Ethiopian Eunuch had of Isaiah when Philip met him (Acts 8:26-28), the person may not have been able to speak or read the language the scroll was written in. The Old Testament was translated from Hebrew to Greek between 280 BC and 250 BC. This is well known today as the Septuagint. The next major translation was the Latin Vulgate (second to fourth century AD). A translation of the New Testament into Arabic did not take place until AD 867. That is 200 years after Muhammad's death in AD 632. Muslim scholars indicate Muhammad could not read, but learned to read through the revelations from Allah through the angel Gabriel. The biography of Muhammad indicates he was not a learned man. So, one must accept one of the following options to reconcile the differences in the Bible and the Quran:

1. Muhammad, the prophet of Islam, did receive his revelation from Allah through Gabriel with all previous Old Testament and New Testament Scripture in error. Truly, the Bible and the Quran as written cannot be reconciled. So, receive the Quran as the Word of Allah and work to earn your salvation (embrace Islam).

2. Muhammad received most of the information regarding the Bible in his travels as a trader by word of mouth with his wives and close acquaintances helping him to record the errors. Those stories with the errors were then recorded in the Quran (reject Islam).
3. Receive the Bible as the Word of the true and living God. Accept Jesus as Lord and Savior who died for your sins (receive Jesus Christ as Lord and Savior).

The selection one would make is critical. It will make the difference in either heaven or hell!

CHAPTER XII
WHAT THE QURAN SAYS ABOUT SALVATION AND ETERNAL LIFE

S alvation is defined as deliverance from sin and from the punishment for sin. The case presented in the Quran is based on man's deliverance of himself. The case presented in the Bible is based on God's deliverance of man. The contrast is stark. One depends on the amount of good deeds accumulated and weighed against the accumulated bad deeds. The other depends on the sin debt being paid by God and the recipient accepting the condition of the payment.

Salvation According to the Quran

The only absolute assurance of a Muslim to reach paradise or heaven is to die as a martyr in a fight against the non-Muslim. Of particular prize inferred in the Quran and the Hadith is the killing of Jews and Christians. A distant second is emigration from the homeland to a non-Muslim country or community in order to further the cause of Islam. In this act, Allah has no binding obligation, but it would significantly count in the good deeds column at the judgment. For Muslims who are not martyred and do not have a relative who was martyred or is not interceded for by Muhammad before Allah, good deeds are the only option. The hope is the good deeds outweigh the bad deeds. With even Muhammad's chief evangelist fearful of Allah's deception and his destiny, and Muslims aware of this history, many desperately try to fulfill all commands given in the Quran and those sighted in the Hadith. Some of the commands from the Quran are given in the following Surah verses:

1. Surah 2:104 (page 42): "And perform the prayer, and pay the alms; whatever good you shall forward to your souls' account, you shall find it with Allah; assuredly Allah sees the things you do."

2. Surah 2:172-173 (page 50-51): "True piety is this: to believe in Allah, and the Last Day, the angels, the Book, and the Prophets, to give of one's substance, however cherished, to kinsmen, and orphans, the needy, the traveler, beggars, and to ransom the slave, to perform the prayer, to pay the alms."

3. Surah 3:16 (page 75): "The true religion with Allah is Islam."

4. Surah 4:16 (page 102): "Those are Allah's bounds. Whoso obeys Allah and His Messenger, He will admit him to gardens

underneath which rivers flow, therein dwelling forever; that is the mighty triumph."

5. Surah 4:82 (page 112): "Whosoever obeys the Messenger, thereby obeys Allah."

6. Surah 10:23 (page 228):

To the **good-doers** the reward most fair and a surplus; neither dust nor abasement shall overspread their faces. Those are the inhabitants of Paradise, therein dwelling forever. And for those who have earned evil deeds the recompense of an evil deed shall be the like of it; abasement shall overspread them, neither have they any defender from Allah, as if their faces were covered with strips of night shadowy. Those are the inhabitants of the Fire, therein dwelling forever.

7. Surah 11:116 (page 252): "And perform the prayer at the two ends of the day and night; surely the **good deeds will drive away the evil deeds**. That is a remembrance unto the mindful. And be thou patent; Allah will not leave to waste the wage of the good-doers."

8. Surah 14:28 (page 277): "As for the evildoers, for them awaits a painful chastisement; but as for those who believe, and do deeds of righteousness, they shall be admitted to gardens underneath which rivers flow, therein dwelling forever by the leave of their Lord, their greeting therein: 'Peace!'"

9. Surah 24:55: "Perform the prayer, and pay the alms, and obey the Messenger – haply so you will find mercy."

10. Surah 5:98 (page 143): "Allah has appointed the Kaaba, the Holy House, as an establishment for men, and the holy month (Ramadan), the offering, and the necklace – that, that you may know that Allah knows all that is in the heavens and in the earth, and that Allah has knowledge of everything."

11. Surah 2:138 (page 46): "Turn thy face towards the Holy Mosque (Kabba). This deals with the daily prayers of the Muslim and the direction the prayers are to be submitted."

12. Surah 22:26-30 (page 30): "And when We settled for Abraham the place of the House (Kabba): Thou shall not associate with Me anything. And do thou purify My house for those that shall go about it and those that stand, for those that bow and prostrate themselves; and proclaim among men the Pilgrimage..."

13. Surah 2:183 (page 52): "The month Ramadan, wherein the Koran was sent down to be a guidance to the people, and a clear signs of the Guidance and the Salvation So let those of you, who are present at the month, fast it."

From the Aforementioned Surah Verses, the Five Pillars of Islam are Derived:

I. The testimony of faith (*Shahadah*): "There is no true god but Allah and Muhammad is the

Messenger (Prophet) of Allah." This is said to be the most important of the Pillars.

II. Prayer (*Salah*): Muslims are to perform prayer five times per day facing toward the Kaaba.

III. Pay the Alms, Giving (*Sakat*): Muslims are to give a certain percentage of what they have held in their position for a lunar year to the poor and needy.

IV. Fasting (*Sawin*): Every year in the month of Ramadan, all Muslims fast from dawn until sundown, abstaining from food, drink, and sexual relations. The Ramadan lasts between twenty-nine and thirty days and begins with the sighting of the first crescent moon of a new moon. The month is the ninth month of the Islamic calendar, which is a lunar calendar. Because the timing is dependent on the lunar phases, the beginning can be as early as April and end as late as September. The month of Ramadan is said to be the month Allah revealed the Quran to Muhammad.

V. The Pilgrimage to Mecca (Makkah), Saudi Arabia (*Hajj*): This is an obligation once in a lifetime for those who are physically and financially able to go. Those who visit the Kaaba are supposed to circle it seven times between the hillocks of Safa and Marwa where Hagar, Ishmael's mother, supposedly searched for water. After the seven times, the pilgrims stand together and ask Allah for what they want and for Allah's forgiveness.

The five pillars of Islam taken individually would indicate the necessity for faith, faith in one god Allah and his messenger Muhammad first and foremost, followed by works in the remaining four pillars. How to pray and the direction of prayer is specific. The Hadith give more specifics on prayer. Giving to help family and the needy is another work seen in the Islamic world today. The Palestinians on the West Bank adjacent to Israel have received support that would fall into this category. Funds channeled through Hezbollah, Hamas, and the Muslim Brotherhood have been used to galvanize community support for these organizations. Today, Ramadan is widely practiced every year by the 1.7 billion Muslims all over the world and about two million Muslims make the Pilgrimage to Mecca each year. Muslims enjoy great latitude in their religious practices all over the world, but do not tolerate other religions, especially in nations that are deemed Islamic and practice Sharia Law.

Attempts to Correlate the Quran to the Bible

There is no question the religion of Islam does not accept the deity of Jesus Christ. According to the Quran, Jesus was created, not the Creator (Surah 3:82); Jesus was not crucified (Surah 4:155), as this was deceit by Allah; Jesus was only a messenger like other Messengers (Surah 5:79); and Jesus was only the son of Mary, not the Son of God (Surah 3:30). Today, many Muslim scholars use the books of Isaiah and the Gospel of John to infer Muhammad was mentioned in the Bible. Muslim scholars use Isaiah 29:12 to explain how Muhammad was unable to read yet received and wrote the Quran. (From Islam: "Gabriel commanded Muhammad by saying, 'Read,' he replied. 'I am not learned.'") (From Isaiah 29:12: "And the book is delivered to him who is not learned, saying, 'Read this, I pray thee;' and he saith, 'I am not learned.'") The context here is God's discipline of Jerusalem and Judah placing the Israelites into a deep spiritual sleep, not being able to discern either God's Word or His discipline. This is not about a descendent of Ishmael; it is about the Jews. Muslims sight the Gospel of John as the proof Muhammad is the Comforter that Jesus said He would send.

In John 15:26, Jesus said, "But when the Comforter is come, whom I will send unto you from the Father, even the Spirit of truth who proceedeth from the Father, He will testify of me."

In John 16:7, Jesus said, "Nevertheless, I tell you the truth: It is expedient for you that I go away; for if I go not away, the Comforter will not come unto you; but if I depart, I will send him to you." The history of Muhammad activities reveals the opposite of being the spirit of truth. Of course, the Muslim position is there is no Holy Spirit of God.

It is ironic that Muslim scholars will use the prophecies of Isaiah and the Gospel of John to attempt to prove some correlation between the Quran and the Bible. What is ignored and dismissed are the most important points of the prophecy and the Gospel. **For this reason, the Books of Isaiah and John are used to present the Christian message of salvation by grace.**

Salvation Presented from the Books of Isaiah and John

Isaiah 9:6 says, "For unto us a child is born, unto us a son is given, and the government shall be upon his shoulder; and his name shall be called Wonderful, Counselor, the Mighty God, the everlasting Father, The Prince of Peace." How is it that a child is born who is the Mighty God? How is it that a child is born who is the everlasting Father? The answer is simple: Jesus is God in the flesh. He is so much more than the Son of Mary.

Isaiah 53:3-12 is the picture of why God's grace is sufficient, beginning with verse 3: "He is despised and rejected of men a man of sorrows and acquainted with grief and we hid as it were our faces from him; he was despised and we esteemed him not." Verse 4: "Surely he hath borne our griefs, and carried our sorrows; yet we did esteem him stricken, smitten of God and afflicted." Verse 5: "But he was wounded for our transgressions, he was bruised for our iniquities; the chastisement for our peace was upon him, and with his stripes we are healed." Verse 6, "The Lord hath laid on him the iniquity of us all." Verse 12: "He was numbered with the transgressors; and he bore the sin of many, and made intercession for the transgressors."

Who is this that was despised, rejected, wounded for our transgression, bore the sin of many and made intercession for the transgressors. Who is this that is worthy to bear the sin debt for so many? This is the child who was born who is the Mighty God who is the Prince of Peace. With mankind's sin debt hanging over him there can be no peace. Someone had to pay the sin debt for all. Who could be an acceptable sacrifice for paying the sin debt of all? It is God the Son, Jesus Christ, the Prince of Peace.

In Isaiah 53:9: "Yet it pleased the Lord (God the Father) to bruise him; he hath put him to grief. When thou shalt make his **soul an offering for sin,** he shall see his seed, shall prolong his days, and the pleasure of the Lord shall prosper his hand." The Hebrew term here not only indicates the inner nature of man, but also his entire personality. What was the inner nature and personality of Jesus the Son of God at this time? It was that of a tender plant, a root out of a dry ground (Isaiah 53:2), and the suffering servant! The suffering servant was offered once and for all for our sin. Jesus Christ is no longer the suffering servant. That was sacrificed on the cross. His soul was made an offering for all sin. When he comes again the suffering servant in nature and personality will not be displayed other than the wounds he sustained in the crucifixion. The nature of Jesus Christ at his second coming will be that of Lord of Lords and King of Kings. In fact, every knee will bow and every tongue will confess Jesus is Lord to the glory of God the Father (Philippians 2:10-11).

From the Gospel of John, the Identity of Jesus Christ is further revealed: In John 1:1: "In the beginning was the Word and the Word was with God and the **Word was God."** In John 1:14: "And the **Word was made flesh**, and dwelt among us (and we beheld his glory, the glory as the only begotten of the Father), full of grace and truth. Who is God that was made flesh? He is the child that was born, the Mighty God, Jesus Christ. "

If God the Son has paid the sin debt for all mankind, how can a person be reconciled to God? In John 3:16-17, Jesus said, "For God so loved the world, that he gave his only begotten Son that whosoever believeth in him should not perish but have everlasting life. For God sent not his Son into the world to condemn the world, but that the world through him might be saved. This is the picture of God's grace not what man can do to save himself."

Could this be true? Is there any room for deceit like that of Allah who is said to be the best at (*makara*) deceit? Again we find in Isaiah 53:9: "And he (Jesus) made his grave with the wicked, and with the rich in his death, because he had done no violence, neither was any **deceit** in his mouth."

What is odd is Muslims will use parts of a book of the Bible to attempt to draw correlations between the Bible and the Quran, but ignore the portions of the same book that challenge basic Islamic beliefs such as the doctrine and deity of Jesus Christ. However, if one accepts the deity and doctrine of Jesus Christ, the Son of God, then Islam falls apart and is void of truth.

Another emphatic emphasis of salvation by grace comes from the Apostle Paul in his letter to the Church at Ephesus. in Ephesians 2:8-9, the Bible says: "For by grace are ye saved through faith; and that not of yourselves, it is the gift of God – Not of works, least any man should boast." There is no room for interpretation to indicate works by mankind have any part in salvation.

What a Contrast?

The Quran and the Bible do agree on one important issue facing mankind. That issue is the consequences of sin. The difference is how that sin debt is paid. In Islam, the debt is paid for with the leftover good works. Good deeds outweigh the bad deeds. The Bible teaches the sin debt has already been paid by the suffering and sacrifice of Jesus Christ the Son of God. Again, the choice of works unto salvation versus Salvation by grace through faith in Jesus Christ are at opposite polar coordinates.

CHAPTER XIII
WHAT DOES THE QURAN SAY ABOUT THE LAST BATTLE AND THE RESURRECTION?

References to the Resurrection and Judgment of Mankind From the Quran:

What does the Quran and the Hadiths say about the last days, the last battle, the resurrection, and the judgment of mankind? The Quran provides a number of Surah verses on the resurrection and judgment, but is limited on the events leading up to them. The Hadiths provide more detail on the events and those involved in the last days and the last battle. Both references were researched to provide a clearer picture of what Muslims are taught and believe.

Although the Surah verses from the Quran are scattered and are in no way chronological, they can be broken down into three categories. **First, are the**

signs approaching the resurrection day? Some of these signs proclaimed by Muslim teachers today include:

1. The splitting of the moon found in Surah 54:1.
2. A creature (beast) coming out of the earth to speak to those who believe in the signs (Surah 27:82).
3. Smoke appears, coming from heaven (Surah 44:10).
4. The appearance of Gog and Magog to initiate the last battle (Surah 18:94 and Surah 21:96-97).

It is said by some Muslim scholars that the splitting of the moon has already occurred and that it was the landing of man on the moon. Also, Muslim scholars say the creature or beast coming out of the earth has already occurred and that it is the computer, the vehicle by which Islam is being spread. The interesting point of these prophecies or signs by Muhammad is the fulfillment is due to the actions and works of man, not Allah.

The second set of events will result in the end of the world. The earth will be made barren (Surah 18:7-8), the trumpet will blow, and the mountains will be crushed (Surah 69:13-15) and a new earth will appear (Surah 14:48). Although the Bible speaks of great destruction upon the earth during the seven years of tribulation, the events are not the same. The Bible in Revelation 21 does speak of a new heaven and new earth. God gave this message to His Son Jesus Christ who gave it to his angel who gave it to

John (Revelation 1:1). This occurred 525 years before Muhammad and the Quran was written.

The third phase of the end time according to the Quran is the resurrection and judgment. According to the following Surah verses, the trumpet will be blown, the moon will be eclipsed, and the sun and moon will be brought together. Allah will roll up heaven in his right hand and mankind will be resurrected in bodily form as they lived on earth. Surah verses referencing the resurrection follow:

1. Surah 2:106 (page 42): "The Jews say, 'the Christians stand not on anything;' the Christians say, 'The Jews stand not on anything;' yet they recite the book. So too the ignorant say the like of them. Allah shall decide between them on the Day of Resurrection touching their differences."

2. Surah 4:153 (page 123): "There is not one of the People of the Book but will assuredly believe in him before his death, and on the Resurrection Day He (Jesus) will be a witness against them (Christians)."

3. Surah 20:102 (page 346): "On the day the Trumpet is blown; and We shall muster the sinners upon that day with eyes staring, whispering one to another, 'You have tarried only ten nights;' WE know very well what they will say, when the justest of them in the way will say, 'You have tarried only a day.'"

4. Surah 21:43 (page 21): "And We shall set up the **just balances** for the Resurrection Day, so that not one soul shall be wronged anything;

even if it be the weight of one grain of mustard-seed We shall produce it, and sufficient are We for reckoners."

5. Surah 34:66 (page 172): "The earth altogether shall be His (Allah's) handful on the Day of Resurrection, and the heavens shall be rolled up in His right hand."

6. Surah 75:4-15 (page 313):

What, does man reckon We shall not gather his bones? Yes indeed; We are able to shape again his fingers. Nay, but man desires to continue on as a libertine, asking, "When shall be the Day of Resurrection?" But when the sight is dazed and the moon is eclipsed, and the sun and moon are brought together, upon that day man shall say, "whither to flee?" No indeed; not a refuge! Upon that day the recourse shall be to thy Lord. Upon that day man shall be told his former deeds and his nay, man shall be a clear proof against himself, even though he offer his excuses.

These Surah verses clearly point to a resurrection followed by a judgment. The judgment will be based on the Balance Scale of Allah with accrued good and evil to be weighted. Jews and Christians are already determined to be weighted with evil by the witness of Jesus, Son of Mary against them. Their condemnation will be that of Gehenna or hell.

References from Hadith Leading up to the Last Battle:

There are over **fifty minor signs** from the Hadiths that Muslim scholars sight that will occur prior to the last days.[22] These signs from the Hadith give more insight into what Muslims believe the events leading up to the last battle will look like. Some of these minor signs are:

1. A time of tribulation and no fear of Allah.
2. Loss of honesty and authority given to those who do not deserve it.
3. Spread of usury, adultery, fornication, and drinking of alcohol.
4. Widespread and condoning of music.
5. Woman population explode that one man will look after fifty women.
6. Many earthquakes.
7. Jews fighting Muslims.
8. The liar believed and the truthful called a liar.
9. The Euphrates will uncover a mountain of gold.
10. Rise of idolatry and polytheists.
11. The land of the Arabs will return to being a land of rivers and fields.
12. Wild animals communicate with humans and man speaks to his shoe.
13. Only the worst people will be left.
14. Nations will call each other to destroy Islam by any and every means.

---

[22] Hosein "Ten Major Signs of the Last Day – Has One Just Occurred", 2007.

15. The truce and joint Christian-Muslim campaign against a common enemy (at the end all war technology shall become useless) followed by the battle of Armageddon the non-Muslim versus the Muslim.

16. **The last of the minor signs is the appearance of the Mahdi.** This is the event that bridges the minor signs to the ten major signs. *Mahdi* means "guided one." The primary description of the Mahdi comes from the Hadith, not the Quran. According to the Shia sect, the Mahdi is the twelfth Imam, Muhammad Al-muntazar, the Hidden Imam, who disappeared in AD 878. They believe he is alive and will reappear at the end time to lead the Muslim armies. Jesus and the armies of Mahdi conquer the world and force everyone to become Muslims. The Dajjal, the Antichrist of the Muslims, and his force of 70,000 Jews, will be destroyed. In the process, Jesus, son of Mary will kill the pigs, break the crosses, and kill the Jews. After this, Jesus will get married, live forty years, and have children. He will die and be buried next to Muhammad in Medina, Saudi Arabia.

Encyclopedia Britannica writes, regarding the Muslim belief in the Mahdi:

In Islamic eschatology, a messianic, deliverer who will fill the Earth with justice and equity, restore true religion, and usher in a short golden age lasting seven to nine years before the end of the world. The Quran does not mention him, and almost no reliable Hadith attributed to Muhammad concerning the Mahdi can be adduced. Many orthodox Sunni theologians accordingly question Mahdist beliefs.[23]

Major Signs

With the last minor sign being the coming of Mahdi the major signs in Islam are set in motion. They follow:

1. **Appearance of the Dajjal (Muslim Antichrist):**[24] Muslim book 41, Hadith 6995-7034: The false messiah, Masih ad-Dajjal, shall appear with Hugh powers as a one-eyed man with other eye blind and deformed like a grape. He will claim to be Allah and to hold keys to heaven and hell and lead many astray, although believers will not be deceived. His heaven is the believer's hell and his hell is the believer's heaven. The Dajjal would be followed by 70,000 Jews of Isfahan wearing Persian shawls.

A further description of the Dajjal and his demise is recorded in the same Hadith number 7015: He (Dajjal) would come to the people and invite them to a wrong religion and they would affirm their faith

---

[23] Editors of Encyclopedia Britannica, "Mahdi Islamic Concept" Updated May 11, 2015.

[24] Islam & World Events "What does Islam believe about the END?".

in him and respond to him. He would then give command to the sky and there would be rainfall upon the earth and it would grow crops. He (Dajjal) would then walk through the waste land and say to it: "Bring forth your treasures and the treasures would come out and collect themselves before him like the swarm of bees." He would then call a person brimming with youth and strike him with the sword and cut him into two pieces and make these pieces lie at a distance which is generally between the archer and his target. He would then call that young man and he will come forward laughing with his face gleaming with happiness and it would at this very time that Allah would send Christ, son of Mary, and he will descend at the white minaret in the eastern side of Damascus wearing two garments lightly dyed with saffron and placing his hands on the wings of two angels. When he would lower his head, there would fall beads of perspiration from his head and when he would raise it up, beads like peals would scatter from it. Every non-believer who would smell the odor of himself would die and his breath would reach as far as he would be able to see. He would then search for him (Dajjal) until he would catch hold of him at the gate of Ludd and would kill him.

2. **Appearance of Jesus, son of Mary:** The return of Isa, from the second sky to kill Dajjal. From the Muslim Book 43 number 656 Bukahri, narrated by Abu Huraira: "Allah's Apostle said, 'The hour will not be established until the son of Mary descends amongst you as a just ruler; he will break the cross, kill the

pigs, and abolish the Jizya tax.'" Money will
be in abundance so that nobody will accept it.

3. **Gog and Magog and the Last Battle**: This
major sign of the end time will be the wall
which imprisons the nations of Gog (Ya'juj)
and Magog (Ma'juj) will break, and they will
surge forth. Some Islamic scholars, such as
Imran Naxar Hosein, believe the wall began
to crack during the life of Muhammad. This
is supported in the hadith when the prophet
mentions "a hole has been made in the wall
containing the Ya'juj and Ma'juj, indicating
the size of the hole with his thumb and index
finger. Their release will occur forty years
prior to the last judgment. The last battle
(Battle of Armageddon) is also referenced in
Surah 21:96-97. However, nearly all Islamic
teaching concerning the last battle comes
from the Hadith.

Following is the description of the Battle of
Armageddon according to 177 Hadith found in "The
Book Pertaining to the Turmoil and Portents of the
Last Hour" (number 6924) Abu Huraira reported
Allah's Messenger (may peace be upon him) as
saying: the last hour would not come until the Romans
would land at al-A'maq or in Dabiq. An army con-
sisting of the best soldiers of the people of the earth
at that time will come from Medina to counteract
them. When they will arrange themselves in ranks,
the Romans would say: "Do not stand between us and
those Muslims who took prisoners from amongst us.

Let us fight with them;" and the Muslims would say: "Nay, by Allah, we would never get aside from you and from our brethren that you may fight them." They will then fight and a third part of the army would run away, whom Allah will never forgive. A third part of the army which would be constituted of excellent martyrs in Allah's eye, would be killed and the third who would never be put to trial would win and they would be conquerors of Constantinople. And as they would be busy in distributing the spoils of war amongst themselves after hanging their swords by the olive trees, the Satan would cry: "The Dajjal (Islam's antichrist) has taken your place among your family." They would then come out, but it would be of no avail. And when they would come to Syria, he would come out while they would be still preparing themselves for battle drawing up the ranks. Certainly, the time of prayer shall come and then Jesus (peace be upon him), son of Mary would descend and would lead them in prayer. When the enemy of Allah would see him, it would disappear just as the salt dissolves itself in water and if he (Jesus) were not to confront them at all, even then it would dissolve completely, but Allah would kill them by his hand and he would show them their blood on his lance the lance of Jesus Christ.

According to Muslim scholars, the above Hadith is representative of the last battle with Rome representative of nations opposing Islam. The Dajjal is the Muslim antichrist.

The Last Battle (Battle of Armageddon), referenced in Quran (Surah 21:96-97; page 25) states: "There is a ban upon any city that We have destroyed;

till, when Gog and Magog are unloosed, and they slide down out of every slope., and nigh has drawn the true promise, and behold, the eyes of the unbelievers staring: 'Alas for us! We were heedless of this; nay, we were evildoers.'"

Muslims believe Gog and Magog stands for wild and lawless tribes who will break their barriers and swarm through the earth. The believing Muslims will be attacked by the unbelievers from every hill or everywhere on earth. Included in the attackers would be the pagan Orientals, Hindus, and Western Societies. According to Islamic scholars, the end of time battle will occur between the Muslims and the people of Gog and Magog who will consist of the bad Jews (Zionists), and the polytheists from the Trinitarian Christians who worship Jesus and the Holy Spirit beside Allah Almighty, and the idol worshipers from the Hindus, and the Far Eastern Orientals.

4. A huge black smoke cloud will cover the earth.
5. The beast that will come out of the ground to talk to people; Surah 27:82 (page 84): "When the word falls on them, We shall bring forth for them out of the earth a beast that shall speak unto them: Mankind has no faith in Our signs."
6. The sun will rise in the West.
7. Three sinking of the earth, one in the east.
8. Sinking of the earth in the west.
9. Sinking of the earth in Arabia.
10. The second trumpet blow will be sounded, the dead will return to life and a fire will start coming out of Yemen that shall gather

all to Mahshar Al Qiy'aaj (The Gathering for Judgment).

Of great interest is the comparison of the last days from the perspective of both Islam and Christianity. What possibly could be the circumstances, the conditions, the environment where civilization would see great tribulation, witness signs and destruction, real time, never previously witnessed by mankind, and yet plunge headlong into rebellion and self destruction? What could place in man's heart the total disregard of events being witnessed on earth without turning to a savior? To answer some of these questions one must compare what the Bible says about the last days and what the Quran and the Hadith say about the last days.

The order of events from a pre-millennial view point according to the Bible follows:

1. Matthew 24:4-14: Wars, and rumors of wars, famine, pestilence, and earthquakes.
2. 1 Thessalonians 4:13-18: Rapture of the church.
3. Matthew 24:15-21 and Daniel 9:24-27: First three and a half years of Tribulation
   a) Many saved by the witness of Jews who turn to Christ Jesus during the tribulation: Revelation 7
   b) Appearance of the antichrist: Revelation 6
   c) One world government: Revelation 6:1-2
4. Matthew 24:21-27: Great Tribulation, last three and a half years of Daniel's seventieth week.

a) Seal Judgments: Revelation 6, 7: War by the antichrist, famine, and Christians saved during this time are martyred and total calamity on earth.

b) Trumpet Judgments: Revelation 8, 9, 11: Total earthly devastation, the abyss opened to allow fallen angels to actively torment mankind.

c) Rise to power of the Beast (antichrist) and the False Prophet: Revelation 13: Worship of the beast and the two witnesses of God killed by the beast.

d) Satan kicked out of heaven and constrained on earth: Revelation 12:12

e) Bowl Judgments: Revelation 16, 17: Painful sores on man, sea, and fresh water supplies become blood, scorching sun, darkness, and Babylon destroyed.

5. Matthew 24:29-31: The return of Christ Jesus to Earth.

6. Revelation 19: The Last Battle, The Battle of Armageddon.

7. Revelation 20: The Great White Throne judgment.

When comparing the events spelled out in the Bible to those in the Quran and the Hadith in a high-level chart form, one can see the two different perspectives force a showdown, the final crisis.

Christianity (Bible)	Islam (Quran & Hadith)	Comments
Wars, famine, earthquakes	Minor signs: tribulation, earthquakes, idolatry and polytheists	
Rapture of the church	The appearance of the Muslim antichrist (Dajjal)	
First 3.5 years of Tribulation; appearance of the antichrist; **one world government**.	The Appearance of the 12th Imam "Mahdi." The return of the Muslim-Christ. **One world religion, Islam, is forced on all civilization**	One world government; Babylon the Great; political, commercial, religious

Second 3.5 years of Great Tribulation with the delivery of the Seal Trumpet and Bowl Judgments; the rise of the beast and false prophet slaying of the two witnesses; Judgment of Babylon	The Muslim antichrist, the "Dajjal," slain with a spear by the Muslim-Christ, Jesus son of Mary. Signs 4 through 9 leading to great events in the heavens and on the earth taking place.	
The return of Jesus Christ with a host from heaven. The destruction of the Beast and False Prophet and those who persecuted Jewish and Gentile Christians; The Battle of Armageddon	The last battle with Muslims against Jews, Christians, and all non-Muslims; The Battle of Armageddon	

The Great White Throne Judgment	The tenth major sign: the gathering for judgment	Muhammad will be the only inter- cessor accept- able to Allah Volume 9, Book 93, Number 601: Bukhari

First, one could conclude **a one world religion of Islam would be a one world government**. There is no separation of politics and government in the religion of Islam.

Second, a Muslim-Christ who would help install a one world religion would be viewed by Christians as the antichrist, not the Jesus son of Mary and defi- nitely not Jesus, God the Son.

Third, the slaying of the Dajjal by the Muslim- Christ could be viewed as the slaying of the two Christian witnesses by the Beast.

Fourth: The belief of Muslims is they will fight the last battle against all non-Muslims (Jews, Christians, all unbelievers of Islam). Christians believe that Jesus Christ will return and lead a host from heaven and defeat and destroy the Beast, False Prophet, and those who persecuted Christians, Jews, and Gentiles. Given these totally opposing beliefs culminating in the last battle, no wonder the Bible prophecy indicates there will be no repentance of those led by the Beast and False Prophet. Death and destruction will reign because both sides. Muslims and Christians believe they are on the right side. In the mean time, hundreds of millions of people die and go to hell.

Of course, the right side has been the question since the crusades. So, when one looks at the commonality of deity and themes involved, what will be the choices and decision made by the concerned?

1. Who is the God of all creation who is Holy, truthful, caring, and loving? The God of the Bible or Allah of the Quran? They are not the same!

2. Who is the Messiah? Jesus the Son of God, God in the Flesh, or Jesus Son of Mary—only a Messenger!

3. What role does Satan play in the end times? Is Satan using the Bible or the Quran to manipulate mankind into hell?

4. What is the inspired word without error and not corrupted? The Bible or the Quran?

5. How can one be assured of salvation? Will a person trust in what they can do to *earn* salvation hoping the scales tip in their favor or will a person receive salvation by grace through faith in the Lord Jesus Christ?

The choices determine one's eternal destiny.

CHAPTER XIV
WHAT IS SHARIAH OR SHARIA LAW?

Fundamental Sharia law is the control and enforcement arm of Islam. There is no such condition of separation of Islam and government. Individual and personal rights are completely trumped by the law. Laws for Muslim women are completely different from Muslim men. Freedom of religion does not exist. In fact, if a person is either born into Islam, or converts to Islam and leaves Islam, the penalty of this religious crime under Sharia Law is death.

Recently, a friend shared the experience her daughter had in Istanbul, Turkey in 2011. As a member of a Christian College student group, with intent to observe the customs and practices of the society, they witnessed Islamic Law in motion. While there they came in contact with a young woman who was being shuffled from place to place by fellow collage friends to hide her from her parents. The young Turkish woman had renounced Islam and become a Christian.

As a result, her relatives were intent on catching her and making her recant or suffer the Islamic law consequences. The nature of this type of consequence is not necessarily carried out by any government agency, but is widely encouraged and accepted as part of Islam.

In Islamic-dominated societies, the arm extends deep into the lives of non-Muslims. If non-Muslims are tolerated at all, they are subjugated to having no status in the society or the court system. In court proceedings, Non-Muslim witnesses are deemed unreliable and receive no priority. If by chance a non-Muslim were to be the plaintiff and win a settlement they are awarded only a fraction of what a Muslim man would receive.

Sharia means path leading to the watering place. **The content and authority of the law comes from the Quran and the Hadiths**. Sharia Law was a system of law installed during the eighth and ninth century by the religious leaders of Islam. The law is intended for the Muslim society and following Sharia law by the Muslim is fundamental to their religious beliefs. To the Muslim, this is Allah's law. Sharia law was regarded as complete at the end of the ninth century when a number of legal manuals were complete by different Islamic authorities. Following the completion of these legal manuals which captured basic law doctrine, a large number of commentaries were produced, which became the traditional and fundamental Sharia law authority.

When penal laws, laws of transactions and family law, are conducted between Muslims one could take the assessment and discussion by Muslim scholars at face value. However, with the Quran teaching Allah to be the best at *Makara* scheming, lying, and deceit and Muslims taught to do the same to non-Muslims (*taqiyya*) for the advancement of Islam, one could hardly accept anything as reliable from a Muslim speaking of the positive attributes of Sharia Law or government for a non-Muslim. Today, most news media outlets reinforce the narrative of the positive attributes of Sharia Law through the propaganda delivered by some Muslim authority. The reality is, Sharia Law practiced in the strictest since, can be seen by the activities of ISIS and other fundamental Islamic groups. Beheading the infidel, enslaving girls and women as sex objects, taxing and taking the property of the marginal Muslim and the unbeliever are all things Muhammad did to the three Jewish groups when he migrated to Medina in 622. When studying the previous chapters on Muhammad and the unbeliever, no embellishment of today's facts is necessary to properly portray the reality of Islamic law.

Scope of Sharia Law

The scope of Sharia is much broader than the Western legal system. The law regulates a Muslim's relationship to neighbors, the state, as well as religious practices. In Sharia law, there is no such thing as separation of religion and state and no separation of individual liberty from religious obligation. The ritual practices specified in the Quran and expounded on in the Hadiths are an integral part of Sharia law. Commands of complete surrender to Allah, daily prayer, giving, fasting, and pilgrimage usually occur in the first chapters of the legal manuals. Unlike western law, Sharia law is viewed as fixed and unchangeable. The belief in Islam is Sharia law is the divine will from Allah and with the death of Muhammad in 632, Allah's divine will cease to be communicated to mankind. In the Islamic legal system, society does not change or reinterpret the law; the law controls society. Muhammad was the last word in the law during his lifetime. He interpreted, expanded, and applied the commands stated in the Quran as he saw fit.[25]

Sharia Law After Muhammad's Death

With the death of Muhammad, the same approach of law application was carried out by the spiritual leaders of Medina. There was a change during the Umayyad Dynasty in 661. The Caliphate was a large military empire that appointed judges in the different provinces and an organized judiciary system was installed. With the different cultures and societies being absorbed into the empire the law changed from being pure Quranic based law to adopting some elements of Roman and Persian law. From the perspective of many Muslim scholars, the pure Quranic legal principles were polluted. The reaction to the polluted law occurred in the eighth century when these Islamic Scholars began to examine the Umayyad legal practices to see if they met the religious intent of Islam.

Out of the examination came two schools of thought and practice. One maintained that outside the Quranic principles, scholars were free to use

---

[25] Coulson "Shariah- Islamic Law", 2012.

their individual reasoning to understand and apply law. The other insisted the only valid foundation and application of the law came from the Quran and the precedents that Muhammad had previously set. The arguments became a simple question: What was the authority by which the law was established? This difference was mitigated by the Jurist al-Shafii (died in 820). Al-Shafii proposed the law from Allah came only through divine revelation. This revelation had to come from the Quran or the Allah-inspired tradition of Muhammad (the Authentic Hadith). Human reasoning was to be strictly confined to deductive reasoning. The move by al-Shafii greatly influenced the collection and classification of the Hadiths. Many Muslim Scholars accepted the Hadith from Bukhari (died in 870) and Muslims view other sources as fictitious. Al-Shafii's approach formed the basis of Islamic jurisprudence. The steps in interpretation, expanding, and applying the law were:

1. Consult the Quran and the Sunnah Hadith (the life and examples of Muhammad's judgments).
2. If no divine answer is revealed, use analogy.
3. Use consensus. If only one judge came to a conclusion, it was deemed conjecture. If there was unanimous agreement by qualified scholars, it was deemed Allah's Law.

Sharia Law differs significantly between Sunni and Shiite Muslims. The Shiite Muslims believe the rulers or Imams are divinely inspired and are therefore spokesmen for Muhammad and can interpret or even give the law. An example of the Shiite approach comes from the supreme leaders of Iran, the Ayatollahs. This is not the case for the Sunni Muslim who would follow the Al-Shafii approach.[26]

Traditional Sharia Law

The traditional Sharia laws are divided into those that are between an individual and Allah and those between an individual and others. The laws between the individual and Allah are fundamentally the five pillars of Islam: commitment to and faith in Allah, prayer, paying alms, fasting (Ramadan), and the pilgrimage to Mecca. Subsets of these laws are found in both the Quran and the Hadiths and include details on how and when to pray, how much and who are to receive alms, and the regulations on fasting. Punishment may vary for breaking some of the fundamentals with the exception of apostasy (renunciation of Islam); the fixed punishment for apostasy is death.

Penal laws that deal with applying punishment to an individual for harming another is treated as a civil injury rather than a crime. I was once in a mid-eastern country looking at a newspaper printed in English. A page that caught my eye was one showing a large arena with a man on his knees, hands tied behind his back with another man (not police or military) holding an AK-47 to the back of his head. The man was executed according to the paper for an atrocity against another person. This was retaliation according to Sharia law. Offences committed by a person against

---

[26] Ibid.,3.

another is punishable by retaliation. This can be any-thing from homicide to assault. The perpetrator is subjected to the same treatment as the victim. This is truly the principal of an eye for an eye and a tooth for a tooth.

In addition to the fixed punishment for apostasy, there are six other specific crimes where the punish-ment is fixed:

1. Highway robbery: punishable by death.
2. Theft: hand amputation
3. Extramarital sex: stoning
4. For fornication, the unmarried offender gets 100 lashes; Surah 24:2 (page 46): the forni-cators scourge each one of them with 100 stripes.
5. For unproven accusation of unchastely, the accuser gets eighty lashes. Surah 24:4 (page 46): "And those who cast it up on women in wedlock, and them bring not four witnesses, scourge them with eighty stripes, and do not accept any testimony of theirs ever; those they are ungodly. Save such as repent thereafter and make amends."
6. Drinking any intoxicant: the accused gets eighty lashes.

In other crimes the punishment depends on the ruling of the judge.

Other Sharia laws included in person to person issues are the transactions law and family law. In transactions law, a person must have reached puberty and be mentally capable; otherwise their affairs are managed by a guardian. (Puberty is defined as twelve years of age for boys and nine years of age for girls.) Muhammad consummated his marriage to a six-year-old when she was nine.

Transactions law cover sale, hire, gift, and loan transactions. In family law, fathers have the right to contract their daughter in marriage regardless of age. Only if the woman has been previously married is her consent necessary. Even then the father or guardian must arrange the marriage contract. Husbands have the right to have four wives. The husband has the right to divorce a wife at will, without question by the law. Men are the managers of the affairs of the woman and if a woman either wife or subject to a guardian is disobedient, the man is to admonish, banish them to their couches, and beat them (Surah 4:38, page 105-106). A child is legitimate only if it is conceived in a lawful marriage. In Sunni law, no legal relationship exists between a father and his illegitimate child. However, the law binds the mother to her illegitimate child.[27]

Court Proceedings

Trials are conducted at the discretion of the judge. No trial by jury exists and there in no cross-examination of the witnesses in Sharia Law. Oral testimony of Muslim witnesses is the main admissible evidence. In western societies, forensic science is used to gather information such as fingerprints, blood samples, and DNA. This type of evidence is readily acceptable in western court systems. However, in Sharia Law, this

---

[27] Ibid.,6,7.

type of evidence is rejected in favor of eyewitnesses. Witnesses must be faithful; that is, Muslim and male Muslim witnesses are considered more reliable than female Muslim witnesses. Non-Muslim witnesses are considered unreliable and receive no priority in a Sharia court. The obstacles before a non-Muslim in a sharia court are near insurmountable. The prospect for a non-Muslim to get a fair trial in a sharia court of law would be slim to none. Another lopsided treatment of a non-Muslim in a Sharia court deals with the sentencing. Sharia courts treat Muslim men different from Muslim women and non-Muslims different from Muslim men. Plaintiff compensation entitlements on a fractional basis of what a Muslim man might receive are:

1. Muslim women would receive half of what a Muslim man would receive.
2. Christians and Jews would receive half of what a Muslim man would receive.
3. Buddhists, Hindus, and Atheists would receive one-sixteenth of what a Muslim man would receive.

The ratios or percentages listed above may vary from court to court, but as a lower percentage.[28]

Freedom of Speech and Religion

Blasphemy in Islam is any form of profanity, questioning Allah or Muhammad, as well as questioning anything that would be considered sacred in

---

[28] Ibid.,10.

Islam. Therefore, to question the origin of Allah, the authority of Muhammad, or the delivery of the Quran would be blasphemy. Punishment for blasphemy ranges from imprisonment, fines, and flogging, to amputation, hanging, and beheading. In some cases, Sharia law allows a non-Muslim to escape death by converting to Islam.

In October 2016, the World Watch Monitor, a news service focused on global persecution of Christians provided an update on the death sentence of Asia Bibi, a Christian mother in Islamabad, Pakistan.[29] Bibi was imprisoned and sentenced to death by hanging for allegedly blaspheming the Muslim prophet Muhammad. Bibi has been imprisoned for seven years awaiting the final trial. Even if pardoned or found not guilty, Islamic clerics have called for Bibi's execution. In today's world, this is a real example of Sharia law at work.

There is no freedom of religion within Sharia law. A person who converts to Islam receives all the benefits any Muslim would have under Sharia law. However, if that person desired to leave or renounce Islam, their punishment would be death. For a person who is deemed an infidel or unbeliever, Sharia law demands they be offered the choice to convert to Islam. If they decline, they are required to pay the tax. If they do not pay the tax, they may be enslaved, killed, or ransomed. A recent article in the *New York Times* outlines the taxes imposed by ISIS in one of

---

[29] The Baptist Record Editor, "Extremists demand Christian's execution" 2016.

the seized areas.[30] There were taxes levied against women, farmers, non-Sunnis, residents of Raqqa, and drivers. The taxes levied against a Shiite or non-Muslim was $200-$2,500, four times per year. Of course, the article presented this as a revenue generator for the leaders of ISIS rather than a part of traditional Sharia law. This law is explicit and found in Surah 9:29 (page 210):

> Fight those who believe not in Allah and the last day and do not forbid hat Allah and his messenger have forbidden – such men as practice not the religion of truth, being of those who have been given the Book (Quran) – until they pay the tribute out of hand and have been humbled.

Fundamental Islam as stated in the Quran demands all apostates and infidels (people of other religions) be put to death, enslaved, or ransomed. This does not leave any room for freedom of speech and freedom of religion. Sharia law is not compatible with a free and democratic society.

---

[30] Almukhtar, "Life Under the Islamic State: Fines, Taxes and Punishments" 2016.

EPILOGUE
WHAT A COMPARISON

When a comparison is made between the Quran and the Bible in either historic content, statements of fact, or doctrine—there is no reconciliation. So, in today's world, how does a religious novice find the truth? In the past fifteen years, there has been a significant push to normalize Islam in the United States through the media and college campus events. For example: while doing research at Purdue University in 2006, I picked up some pamphlets advertising Islamic Awareness week. The pamphlets were provided by the Institute of Islamic Information and Education in Chicago, Illinois. They were distributed by Muslim students. Quoting from the pamphlet, "Introduction to Islam:"

> Muhammad is considered to be the summation and the culmination of all prophets and messengers that came before him. He purified the previous messages from adulteration

and completed the message of Allah for humanity. He was entrusted with power of explaining, interpreting and living the teachings of the Quran.

Another pamphlet titled, "Muhammad in the Bible" states, "It was prophet Muhammad (peace be upon him) who was the paraclete, comforter, helper, admonisher sent by Allah after Jesus ... He did reprove the world of sin, of righteousness and of Judgment (John 16:8-11)." Again, what would the novice think if they had no biblical background and did not know this spoke of the Holy Spirit?

Could the Quran be Accepted at Face Value?

The novice could accept the Quran at face value without considering the history of Muhammad's life. However, even a novice would want to know answers to some questions: Would Muhammad be righteous enough to be placed in the position of being the only religious spokesman to all humanity? Would he be righteous enough to reprove the rest of the world of sin? Would he be elevated to the position of being next to Allah? Muhammad was unlearned, and with a limited education. Yet, he was intelligent, tenacious, charismatic, scheming, deceitful, and ruthless.

These well-known facts are illustrated by the following historical examples: He seized two of the three Jewish group's land and possessions and expelled them after being welcomed by these people when he migrated to Medina in 624. Shortly thereafter, he beheaded 800 men and boys of the third Jewish group (these were the Banu Qurazas). He made slaves of the women and children and sexual slaves of the more appealing women. Muhammad took Rayhana bint Zayd as his personal sex slave in 627; her husband being one of the 800 Muhammad beheaded.

Another example is when Muhammad pressured his adopted son, Zayab, to divorce his wife so that he could marry her. Muhammad married Zaynab bint Jahsh, his biological cousin, in 627 and proclaimed he could have more than four wives because he was a prophet. Muhammad's treatment of women as inferior and his use of sexual slaves are strong indicators of his moral fiber. His attitude, even hatred of Jews and Christians, is prominent throughout the Quran. If the life history of Muhammad is explored, one would have a difficult time accepting him as a model of morality. One would have a difficult time accepting him to be the culmination of all previous prophets, and the one who would purify all previous messages from adulteration. Finally, with Muhammad's sexual and murderous track record, among other things, how could one accept Muhammad to be the one assigned to reprove the world of sin?

Many of the actions in Muhammad's life would be considered sinful according to the Bible. However, a different perspective is gained when looking at the attributes of Allah, the god of Muhammad. The Quran states Allah is the best at (*makara*) scheming, lying, deceiving, double-dealing (Surah 3:46). Muhammad had and exercised these same attributes. So, if Allah is real, it looks like he created Muhammad in his own image.

The Biblical Alternative

One should accept the Bible as the Word of the God of creation. Realizing the word was authenticated through many **miracles** by Old Testament prophets such as Elijah and Elisha. Realizing the word was authenticated by Old Testament prophets such as Isaiah, Jeremiah, Ezekiel, and Daniel, whose prophecies were and are being fulfilled. Realizing the Word was authenticated by Jesus Christ, the Son of God, by the miracles He did and the miracles He empowered His disciples to do. Realizing the best works that man can do to save himself falls woefully short and salvation is by God's grace through faith in the Lord Jesus Christ.

This forces a realization that the Quran is a compilation of verbal biblical stories, with many errors, most likely accumulated by Muhammad in his travels and dealings as a merchant. Taking these verbal exchanges and adding his own bias, Muhammad created a religion to fit his agenda that galvanized and directed his followers.

Two questions to pose concerning Muhammad: Did Muhammad truly believe he was the final messenger of Allah, or did Muhammad create Allah in his own image?

REFERENCES

Chapter I – XV

1. Holy Bible, Authorized King James Version, The New Scofield Study Bible, editor C.I. Scofield, D.D., Oxford University Press, Inc.
2. A.J. Arberry, The Koran Interpreted, a Translation First Touchstone Edition 1996.

BIBLIOGRAPHY

1 National Counter Terrorism Center, "Historic TimeLine 1969-2001" http://www.nctc.gov/site/timeline.html.

2 Shaykh al-Hadith, Allama Ghulam Rasul Saidi, "Imam Bukhari (194-265)", trans. Allamah Ishfaq Alam Qadri and M. Iqtidar, http://sunnah.org/history/scolars/imam-bukhari.htm.

3 Mohamed Okasha, "Al Bukhari: The Imam of Hadith and Sunnah" The Faith, August 4, 2015, accessed December 22, 2016, http://www. The-faith.com/Islamic-history/albukhari-thep-imam-of hadith-and-sunnah.

4 Viviene Walt, "Meet the Woman the Paris Gunman Spared", Time, Updated January 9, 2015, http://www.time.com/3661222/charlie-hebdo-woman-gunman-spared.

5 Salatomatic, "Mosques and Islamic Schools", http://www.Salatomatic.com/reg/united-states/.

6   Seyyed Hossein Nasr, "Muhammad Prophet of Islam", Encyclopedia Britannica, last updated June 23,2016, accessed November 5, 2016, http://www. Britannica.com/biography/ Muhammad.

7   Allamah Muhammad Baqir, "A detailed biography of Prophet Muhammad -Wives of the Prophet – their number and a brief account of them", accessed December 22, 2016, http:// www.Al-Islam.org.

8   Myriam Francois-Cerrah, "The truth about Muhammad and Aisha", The Guardian, September 17, 2015, accessed December 22, 2016, http://theguardian.com/commentisfree/ belief/2012/sep/17/muhammad-aisha-truth.

9   Michael Lipka, "Muslims and Islam: Key findings in the U.S. and around the world" Pew Research Center, July 22, 2016. accessed December 10, 2016, http://www.pewre-search.org.

10 Todd Johnson, Gina Zurlo, Albert Hickman and Peter Crossing, "Christianity 2015 Religious Diversity & Personal Contact", Gordon-Cromwell Theological Seminary, January 2015. accessed December 20, 2016, http://www.gordonconwell.edu.

11 Editors of Encyclopedia Britannica, "Sin Mesopotamian God" last updated November 22, 2000. accessed December 19, 2016, https://www.britannica.com/topic/ Sin-Mesopotamian-god.

12 Editors of Encyclopedia Britannica, "Palmyra" last updated April 15, 2016, https://www.britannica.com/place/palmyra/syria.

13 Flavius Josephus, trans. William Whiston, "The Works of Flavius Josephus" Volume IV, Antiquities of the Jews, chapter 3, page 11, reprinted 1974.

14 CBS/AP, "Jordanian pilot's "Obscene" burning death by ISIS sparks outrage in Mideast" February 4, 2015. Accessed November 10, 2016, http://www.cbsnews.com//Jordanian -pilot-obscene-burning-death-by-ISIS-sparks -outrage.

15 Laura Smith-Spark and Michael Martinez, "Who was Jordanian pilot Moath al-Kasasbeh, Killed by ISIS" CNN , February 3, 2015, accessed December 20, 2016,http:// www.cnn.com/2015/01/29/middleeast/ who-is-jprdan-pilot-ISIS-hostage/.

16 Patrick Goodenough, "Six Years Later: Obama Finally Calls Fort Hood a Terrorist Attack" CNS News, December 7,2015, accessed August 10, 2016, http://www.cnsnews.com/ news/article/patrick-goodenough/obama-six-years-later-calls-fort -hood-terrorist-attack.

17 Ben Welsh and Tony Barboza, "San Bernardino shooting updates" Los Angeles Times, December 9,2015, accessed September 2016, http://www.latimes.com/local/lanow/ la-me-in-san-bernardino-shooting-live-up-dates-htmistpru.html.

18 CNN Library, "Boston Marathon Terror Attack Fast Facts" updated April 8, 2016, accessed June 2016, http://www.cnn.com/2013/06/03/us/Boston-marathon-terror-attack-fast-facts.

19 Lawrence Mower, "Orlando shooter Omar Mateen was gay, former classmate says" Palm Beach Post, June 14, 2016, http://www.PalmBeachPost.com.

20 Kim Willsher, "Hasna Aitboulahcen: police examine remains of 'cowgirl' turned suicide bomber" The Guardian, Nowember 20, 2015, accessed December 21, 2016, http://www.theguardian/world/2015/nov/20/hasna-ait-boulahcen-party-girl-who-became-paris-suicide-bomber.

21 National Counter Terrorism Center, "Historic TimeLine 2000-2015".

22 Imran Nazar Hosein, "Ten Major Signs of the Last Day – Has one Just Occurred" Wednesday, 10 Rajab 1428 (year 2007), accessed July 28, 2016, http://www.iranhosein.org/articles/signs-of-tje-last-day/76-ten-makpr-signs-of-last-d.

23 Editors of Encyclopedia Britannica, "Mahdi Islamic Concept" updated May 5, 2015, accessed October 10, 2016, http://www.britannica.com/topic/mahdi.

24 Islam & World Events, "What does Islam believe about the End?" Truth Network, July 28, 2016 accessed August, 2016, http://www.truthnet.org/islam/Islam-Bible/4Islambeliefs/.

25 Noel James Coulson, "Shariah = Islamic Law" Encyclopedia Britannica, Last updated March 20, 2012, accessed August 13,2016. http://www.britannica.com/topic/Shariah.

26 Ibid., 3.

27 Ibid., 6,7.

28 Ibid., 10.

29 William Perkins ed."Extremists demand Christian's execution" The Baptist Record, October 20, 2016, http://www.mbcb.org.

30 Sarah Almukhtar, "Life Under the Islamic State: Fines, Taxes and Punishments" New York Times, May 26,2016, accessed August 2, 2016, http://www.nytimes.com/interactive/2016/05/26/world/middleeact/isis-taxes-fines-revenue.

CPSIA information can be obtained
at www.ICGtesting.com
Printed in the USA
FSOW02n1624300117
30213FS